The Great Tribulation

The Great Tribulation

R. Bradley Jones

BAKER BOOK HOUSE
Grand Rapids, Michigan

ACKNOWLEDGMENTS

The author acknowledges his indebtedness to the following for their generous permission to use quoted material:

Augsburg Publishing House, Minneapolis, Minnesota
Interpretation of Epistle to Hebrews, by R. C. H. Lenski

Baker Book House, Grand Rapids, Michigan
Baker's Dictionary of Practical Theology, edited by E. F. Harrison
The Divine Covenants, by A. W. Pink
Introduction to the Study and Knowledge of the Holy Scripture, by T. H. Horne

Broadman Press, Nashville, Tennessee
Christian Doctrine, by W. T. Conner

Macmillan Company, New York
The Problem of Pain, by C. S. Lewis

Moody Press, Chicago, Illinois
The New Testament, by Charles B. Williams

Wm. B. Eerdmans Publishing Co., Grand Rapids, Michigan
First & Second Epistles of Thessalonians, by Leon Morris
New Bible Dictionary, edited by J. D. Douglas
Prophecy of Daniel, by Edward J. Young
Theological Dictionary of the New Testament, edited by Kittel

Oxford University Press, New York, N. Y.
New Scofield Reference Bible, edited by E. S. English

Presbyterian & Reformed Publishing Co., Nutley, New Jersey
An Eschatology of Victory, by J. Marcellus Kik
Prophecy and the Church, by O. T. Allis

Fleming H. Revell, Nutley, New Jersey
Gospel According to Matthew, by G. Campbell Morgan

Preface

The Lord Jesus, just before going to the cross, told His followers, "In the world ye shall have tribulation: but be of good cheer; I have overcome the world" (John 16:33).

Should we not, therefore, expect tribulation as a part of the regenerate life? Yes. But many Christians fail to remember Jesus' words. If a dedicated Christian suffers much we wonder why or even question the goodness of God. We forget the words of the Lord and remember the promise of some evangelist who told us when we made our profession of faith that that was all we needed to do to be assured of a happy life thereafter. He should have warned us that if we did not at some time suffer for our faith, we should ask ourselves why not. The New Testament surprises us by the many things it says about the believer's suffering for Christ's sake. Indeed, a careful reading of God's Word will convince us that all true Christians shall pass through great tribulation, but emerge from it into the tearless life of eternal joy with the triumphant Christ (Rev. 7:14).

Russell Bradley Jones

Contents

Introduction

Will the church go through the great tribulation? is a question vigorously debated by Bible students today. One familiar with the Scriptures hesitates to ask such a question. It is like asking in time of war, "Will the soldiers engage in conflict?" Our Lord answered the question when He said, "Whosoever doth not bear his cross, and come after after me, cannot be my disciple" (Luke 14:27).

A GREAT TRIAL OF AFFLICTION

The Greek word translated *tribulation* or *affliction* literally means "pressure." It is used of distress brought about by outward circumstances; often of trouble in the spiritual sense. Young's *Concordance* shows that the Greek word *thlipsis* is translated *tribulation* twenty-one times, *affliction* seventeen, *trouble* three times, *anguish* once, and *persecution* once, in the King James Version of the New Testament. And there are other words conveying the same meaning.

These are words describing situations that many modern church-goers like to avoid. The name of the game to them is "escape." Salvation: Doesn't that mean escape from the torments of hell? Service: Doesn't that mean attending the Sunday morning worship service, putting a dollar or so in the collection plate, and singing with neighbors and friends in happy fellowship?

Wait! What did the Lord Jesus mean when He told His disciples, "In the world ye shall have tribulation, but be of good cheer; I have overcome the world" (John 16:33)? Of course there is a very sad and true sense in which this warning applies to all men. As Eliphaz, Job's friend, said, "Man is born unto trouble, as the sparks fly upward" (Job 5:7). But our Lord was not speaking about the troubles that befall sinful men as men, nor the chastisement they receive because of sin; He was speaking of the mysterious sorrows that fall on them because they are believers.

And why is the activity of Paul and his comrades, on their missionary journeys, described as "confirming the souls of the disciples, and exhorting them to continue in the faith, and that we must through much tribulation enter into the kingdom of God"? (Acts 14:22). Cannot we say that the New Testament takes for granted that tribulation is the normal lot of Christians: "No cross, no crown"?

A SEVEN-YEAR GREAT TRIBULATION

Largely ignoring the above Scriptures in their writings, a group of interpreters have neatly packaged almost all really serious trouble during the gospel age into one bundle, which they mislabel the great tribulation. And they postpone it to the last seven years just before or after Jesus comes a second time.

The majority of these interpreters, the pre-tribulationists, answer our question with a positive, "No, the church will not pass through the great tribulation." Another group, known as post-tribulationists, say, "Yes, the church will pass through the great tribulation." There are others who complicate matters by answering, yes and no. The mid-tribulationists hold that the church will pass half way through the great tribulation before the rapture. And the partial-tribulationists tell us that only those who are watching and waiting for Christ's appearing will be raptured and escape the tribulation.

The amazing thing about all this is that it is based on a future *seven-year* tribulation, which is nowhere mentioned or even hinted at in either the Old or the New Testament.

"I object," one of my tribulationist friends interrupts. "The seven year great tribulation is found in Daniel's prophecy of the seventieth week" (Dan. 9:24-27). Then he goes to great lengths to show me that there is a hiatus, or an interval of hundreds of years, between Daniel's sixty-ninth and seventieth week, and the seventieth week is still future. I shall reserve my refutation of this point for a future chapter on tribulation prophesied by Daniel, except to say that the only way you can postpone Daniel's seventieth week to the future is to ignore the crucifixion of our Savior and invent an indefinite period of centuries and wedge it in, without rhyme or reason, between the sixty-ninth and the seventieth. If you can so violate the simple rules of Scriptural interpretation, you can make the Bible teach anything you want it to teach.

If this objector reminds me of our Lord's Olivet prophecy in Matthew 24, Mark 13, and Luke 21:5-36, and points to the words, "Then shall be great tribulation," I will still insist that there is not a word in those references about a *seven-year* tribulation. And I will point out that history proves that that particular tribulation was experienced by the Jews when the Romans destroyed Jerusalem in A.D. 70.

"But," argues my objector, "you are forgetting the law of double reference, which says:

> The same prophecies frequently have a double meaning, and refer to different events, the one near, the other remote; the one temporal, the other spiritual or perhaps eternal. The prophets thus having several events in view, their expressions may be partly applicable to one, and partly to another, and it is not always easy to make the transition. What has not been fulfilled in the first, we may apply to the second, and what has already been fulfilled, may often be considered as typical of what remains to be accomplished."[1]

---

[1]Thomas Hartwell Horne, *An Introduction to the Critical Study and Knowledge of the Holy Scriptures.* 5 vols. 8th ed. (Grand Rapids: Baker, 1970), Vol. II, p. 540.

This so-called law of double reference is no law at all. It is a means of adapting the plain prophecies of Scripture to whatever preconceived notions the interpreter may have. An authority on scriptural interpretation says of this "law":

> There has arisen not only the doctrine of a double sense, but of a threefold and fourfold sense, and the rabbis went so far as to insist that there are "mountains of sense in every word of Scripture." . . . The moment we set forth the principle that portions of Scripture contain an occult or double sense we introduce an element of uncertainty in the sacred volume, and unsettle all scientific interpretation. . . . Says Ryle, "I hold that the words of Scripture were intended to have one definite sense, and that our first object should be to discover that sense, and adhere rigidly to it. . . . To say that words *do* mean a thing merely because they *can* be tortured into meaning it is a most dishonorable and dangerous way of handling Scripture." "This scheme of interpretation," says Stuart, "forsakes and sets aside the common laws of language."[2]

THE TRIBULATION, THE GREAT

Here we must take note of a surprising fact, for it is bound to influence the answer to our question of whether the church will pass through the great tribulation.

In the Greek New Testament, the designation "great tribulation" is modified by the definite article only twice. And these two times are in one reference: Revelation 7:14. "These are the ones coming out of *the* tribulation, *the* great, and have washed their robes and whitened them in the blood of the Lamb." Notice that the definite article is repeated: *the* tribulation, *the* great. This is more significant than the average English reader may realize.

Dr. A. T. Robertson, New Testament Greek authority, says, "The (definite) article is never meaningless in the Greek. . . . The article is associated with gesture and aids in pointing out like an index finger. . . . Wherever the Greek article occurs, the object is

---

[2]M. S. Terry, *Biblical Hermeneutics*, 1885, p. 383.

certainly definite."[3] To illustrate: *A* savior may be one of many so-called saviors; *the* Savior means the one and only Savior.

Since all the other references to a great tribulation in the Greek New Testament lack the definite article, we must remember that *the tribulation, the great* in Revelation 7:14 comprehends all the other tribulations wherever mentioned. And since John pictures the final gathering of all the redeemed "before the throne of God," who "have washed their robes, and made them white in the blood of the Lamb," and describes them as "coming out of the tribulation, the great," we have the answer to our question. They are the blood-washed from "all nations, and kindred, and people, and tongues" (v. 9). Here are all the redeemed gathered home with their Lord and Savior. And every one of them has passed through "the tribulation, the great."

Now, let us go on to see how Scripture verifies the affirmations of this introduction.

[3]A. T. Robertson, *A Grammar of the Greek New Testament in the Light of Historical Research* (Nashville: Broadman, 1934), p. 756.

Tribulation's Genesis

Tribulation is the common experience of mankind. "Man that is born of woman is of few days, and full of trouble," says the Book of Job, one of the oldest if not the oldest book of the Bible. And the last book of the Bible describes redeemed man's earthly experience as "the tribulation, the great." Not even the followers of the Lord Jesus escape this common experience of mankind. He promised His own, "In the world ye shall have tribulation, but be of good cheer; I have overcome the world" (John 16:33).

CONTRIBUTING FACTORS

Why does man suffer trials and tribulations? The three-fold answer is simple: The sovereign Creator demands loving obedience of those created in His own image. The evil adversary of God tempts man into disobedience to his Maker. And free man chooses to make self his god, thereby separating himself from the true God and becoming the servant of Satan. The record of all this is in the first three chapters of Genesis.

The Sovereign God of the World

⸜ From other Scriptures we learn of the true God's omnipresence (Ps. 139:8–10), His omniscience (Acts 15:18), and His omnipotence (Rom. 13:1). We also learn that God is holy (Exod. 15:11), perfect (Matt. 5:48), and loving (I John 4:16).

Furthermore, we are told of an extraordinary council convened by the Trinity "before the foundation of the world" in Ephesians 1:4–10, at which time it was revealed that God had

> chosen us [future believers] in him [Christ]. . . that we should be holy and without blame before him in love: having predestinated us unto the adoption of children by Jesus Christ to himself, according to the good pleasure of his will, to the praise of the glory of his grace, wherein he hath made us accepted in the beloved. In whom we have redemption through his blood, the forgiveness of sins according to the riches of his grace; wherein he hath abounded toward us in all wisdom and prudence; having made known unto us the mystery of his will, according to his good pleasure which he hath purposed in himself: that in the dispensation of the fulness of times he might gather together in one all things in Christ, both which are in heaven, and which are on earth, even in him.

In this unique revelation, we discover: (1) God's purpose in creating the world and mankind was ultimately to bring into existence a redeemed family for His eternal enjoyment. (2) God's problem was the saving and purifying of man from sin which would result from the first man's foreseen evil choice. (3) God's method of accomplishing His purpose was to demonstrate His good pleasure and grace by pouring out His blood in the person of His Son.

This cannot mean that God is the author of evil. But as a loving Father He uses the chastening rod to reveal the consequence of sin and to turn man to Christ.

The Evil Adversary of God

The adversary, Satan, garbed in the flesh of a beautiful serpent, soon presents himself to the newly created man. He boldly attacks the integrity of the Creator, and ever after appears as His enemy. Who was he? What was his origin? The Bible gives no clearly certain answer. His presence in the world is permitted by God; he is limited by the wise purposes of the Creator; and he will experience everlasting damnation.

> In the realm of free moral character building, evil must be a possibility or good must be an impossibility. Free moral character is the strength acquired in the conflict with evil.... It takes the sufferings in the conflict with sin's encroachment to make the saint. Instead of untried innocence, man is to be possessed with intelligent and victorious experience, the Godlike faculty of perfect moral knowledge. When man has fought his way back through faith, by grace, to a chosen chastity and a voluntary virtue from the bonds of sin, he will know what his untried brother can never fully know. He will be able to sing a song of redemption in which even angels cannot join.[1]

The Free Man's Choice

"God created man in his own image, in the image of God created he him; male and female created he them" (Gen. 1:27). And God gave man "dominion . . . over every living thing that moveth upon the earth" (Gen. 1:28). Man was made in God's image and given dominion over the earth, therefore man was free.

The original man's position was unique. He was innocent of wrong doing. "Adam had no evil ancestry behind him, no corruption within him, nothing in his body to distress him.... He was, nevertheless, a creature, and as such subject unto the authority of the One who had given him being."[2]

The fact that man was also in circumstances of probation appears in Genesis 2:16–17: "The Lord God commanded the man, saying, Of every tree of the garden thou mayest freely eat: but of the tree of knowledge of good and evil, thou shalt not eat of it, for in the day that thou eatest thereof thou shalt surely die."

Of this portion of Scripture G. Campbell Morgan wrote:

---

[1] T. H. Nelson, *The Bible Champion*, 36 (March 1930): 114.
[2] A. W. Pink, *The Divine Covenants* (Grand Rapids: Baker, 1973), p. 34.

It was for man to choose whether he would abide in that relation to God, which would assure his fullest realization of possibil-
ity, or whether he would by severance from God encompass his
own ruin. It was a terrible and awful alternative. Yet unless it
were offered to man, the highest fact of his being would be at-
rophied, for will power, having no choice, ceases to be of value.
He was a sovereign under a Sovereign; independent, but depen-
dent. He had the right of will, but this could only be perfectly
exercised in perpetual submission to the will of God.[3]

Man, the privileged creature of God, violated his probation,
renounced his responsibility, exercised his independence, separated himself from God, and opened the door to suffering and
tribulation.

All mankind was actually and potentially present in the one
person Adam when he violated his probation and fell. Therefore
his apostasy was actively and voluntarily the apostasy of the
whole human race; and his condemnation was justly and logi-
cally the condemnation of the whole human race (Rom. 5:12–
21).

EARLY EXPANSION

When Adam broke his relationship to the loving heavenly
Father, God was immediately faced with a double problem: re-
gaining that love relationship and at the same time remaining
true to His character as the perfectly righteous Creator. God's
righteousness must react against sin and condemn it. God's love
must redeem the sinner, cleanse him of his sin, and begin the
process of restoring His image in him. God both loves and condemns him. "This is not to affirm an inconsistency in God; the
inconsistency is in man. God loves man because of his worth
and condemns him because of his unworthiness."[4]

From the time of the fall of Adam until the call of Abram, the
Father reacted to man's disobedience in three ways: Man's ex-

---

[3]G. Campbell Morgan, *The Crises of the Christ* (New York: Revell, 1903).
[4]W. T. Conner, *Christian Doctrine* (Nashville: Broadman, 1937), p. 95.

pulsion from the garden, man's destruction by the flood, and the confusion of man's tongue at Babel.

Man's Expulsion from the Garden

The initiative in the tragic drama of mankind's fall was taken by the Lord God of grace. "And the Lord God called unto Adam, and said unto him, Where art thou? . . . Hast thou eaten of the tree, whereof I commanded thee that thou shouldest not eat? . . . What is this that thou hast done?" (Gen. 3:9, 11, 13) These questions must have shocked the man and the woman into a realization of their fearful condition in sinful disobedience. Then follows the Lord's announcement of predetermined grace and of consequent tribulation, first in words, then in symbolic action.

Addressing the serpent as the slave of Satan, the Lord God said, "I will put enmity between thee and the woman, and between thy seed and her seed; it shall bruise thy head, and thou shalt bruise his heel" (Gen. 3:15). The heel of the Seed of the Woman would be injured painfully, while He was fatally crushing the head of the serpent's seed. This prophecy is called the *protevangelium*, or the first announcement of a Savior. It indicated that there would be continuous conflict between Satan and mankind involving suffering. Further revelations would gradually clarify the full meaning of this promise.

Furthermore, the earthly future would be marked by sorrow and pain both for the woman (Gen. 3:16) and for the man (Gen. 3:17–19) as a consequence of their disobedience. This visitation of sorrow and pain would prove to be a merciful provision of a loving God. It was, as the Lord said, "For thy sake" (Gen. 3:17), or "for thy good." Sorrow, toil, and pain would be turned into an instrument for spiritual development. "For godly sorrow worketh repentance to salvation not to be repented of" (II Cor. 7:10).

C. S. Lewis writes,

We are not merely imperfect creatures who must be improved; we are rebels who must lay down our arms. The first answer, then, to the question why our cure should be painful, is that to render back the will which we have so long claimed for our own, in itself is, wherever and however, it is done, a grievous pain. . . . But pain insists upon being attended to. God whispers to us in our pleasures, speaks in our conscience, but shouts in our pain: it is His megaphone to rouse a deaf world. . . . No doubt pain as God's megaphone is a terrible instrument; it may lead to final and unrepented rebellion. But it gives the only opportunity the bad man can have for amendment. It removes the veil; it plants the flag of truth within the fortress of a rebel soul. And that is why tribulations cannot cease until God either sees us remade or sees that our remaking is now hopeless.[5]

Following God's words of justice and love, "The Lord God did make coats of skins, and clothed them" (Gen. 3:21). This symbolic action revealed that another (in this case an animal) could substitute for the sinner in providing covering (atonement), but only by the death of the substitute.

Patrick Fairbairn, authority on typology, says,

Surely it is not attributing to the venerable heads of the human family, persons who had so recently walked with God in paradise, an incredible power of spiritual discernment, or supposing them to stretch unduly the spiritual import of this particular action of God, if we should conceive them turning the divine action into a ground of obligation and privilege for themselves, and saying, here is heaven's own finger pointing out the way of obtaining relief to our guilty consciences: the covering of our shame is to be found by means of the skins of irrational creatures, slain in our behalf: *their* life for *our* lives, their clothing innocense for *our* shame; and we cannot err, we shall but show our faith in the mercy and forgiveness we have experienced, if, as often as the sense of shame and guilt returns upon our consciences, we follow the footsteps of the Lord, by a renewed sacrifice of life, clothe ourselves with His own appointed badge of acquittal and acceptance.[6]

An additional act of justice and love on the part of God, combining punishment and protection, is recorded in Genesis 3:22–

---

[5]C. S. Lewis, *The Problem of Pain* (New York: Macmillan, 1965), pp. 93–94.
[6]Patrick Fairbairn, *The Typology of Scripture* (New York: Funk & Wagnalls, 1900), Vol. I, p. 250.

24. The last verse of this passage reads, "So he drove out the man; and he placed at the east of the Garden of Eden Cherubims, and a flaming sword which turned every way, to keep the way of the tree of life."

This was an act of justice, because man must know that a God-pleasing and eternal life cannot be enjoyed in a state of disobedience; yet it was also an act of love, because if man returned to the garden and to the tree of life, which had the power of sustaining immortality, and in this case the immortality of depraved flesh, he would have faced disastrous consequences under the curse of God. This action of the Lord impressed man's mind that he had been turned from his proper habitation to an existence from which he, as one made in the image of God, must escape into true blessedness.

Did this first pair of sinners understand this primitive gospel? Yes, Genesis 3:20 implies that they did: "Adam called his wife's name Eve, because she was the mother of all living." Eve means life. Does not this indicate that as far as it was possible under the circumstances, Adam exercised a true faith that the Seed born of Eve would win the victory over the serpent's brood?

It is interesting to see that Abel in his worship of God, brought "the firstlings of his flock" and offered them, an act surely reminiscent of God's slaying of animals to cover the nakedness of his parents. And "The Lord had respect unto Abel and his offering" (Gen. 4:4). Hebrews 11:4 adds, "By faith Abel offered unto God a more excellent sacrifice than Cain, by which he obtained witness that he was righteous, God testifying of his gifts." This faith was surely the result of the parental teaching in that early family circle.

Man's Destruction by the Flood

Three sons of Adam and Eve are mentioned in the biblical record: Cain, Abel, and Seth. Abel, as we have seen, proved to be a man who sought to please God. Strangely his worship of God displeased his brother Cain, whose worship ignored the revealed will of God and exalted self. Instead of repenting at God's rebuke he became angry with Abel and slew him (Gen.

4:5–8). Thus began the active enmity of the world against the people of God.

Cain became a "fugitive and a vagabond in the earth" (Gen. 4:12). Seven of his descendants are named, only two of whom seem to give evidence by their names (Mehujael and Methusael) of some parental recognition of God. Cain built a city. The sixth generation from Cain produced Lamech, who became a bigamist and a boasted murderer. Devotion to things, such as cattle, music, brass and iron, seems to have claimed the interest of others of Cain's line. These proved themselves unworthy of bearing the line of the Seed of the Woman, and nothing more is said of them, except where Cain is mentioned as an example of ungodliness (Heb. 11:4; I John 3:12; Jude 11).

Abel apparently died without issue. When Seth, a third son, was born to Adam, Eve named him "Appointed" or "Substitute," again giving evidence of faith in God's promise.

About a thousand years elapsed, according to the chronology of Genesis 5, from Adam to Noah, with ten heads of families in the line. Seth, the third son of Adam, was one of these family heads. Only a relatively small number of these were worthy of memory as servants of the Lord: Enos (Gen. 4:26), Enoch (Gen. 5:22, Heb. 11:5, Jude 14–15), and Noah (Gen. 5:29). Others, less prominent, may have been as devout, for Seth's line was the bearer of the Seed of the Woman.

Adam's two lines of descendants seem to have developed in different directions: the Cainites observed the ways of self and the world, while the Sethites for a long time were more devoted to God. However, the two streams began to commingle (Gen. 6:1–4), with the obliteration of moral distinctions as a result. This endangered the standing of the Sethites as the bearer of the promised Seed of the Woman.

> God saw that the wickedness of man was great in the earth, and that every imagination of the thoughts of his heart was only evil continually. And it repented the Lord that he had made man on the earth, and it grieved him at his heart. And the Lord said, I will destroy man whom I have created from the face of the earth, both man, and beast, and the creeping thing, and the fowls of the air; for it repenteth me that I have made them (Gen. 6:5–7).

"But Noah found grace in the eyes of the Lord. . . . Noah was a just man and perfect in his generations, and Noah walked with God" (Gen. 6:8–9). With him the Lord established a covenant, making Noah the head of a new line to bear the Seed of the Woman. After a probation period of 120 years (Gen. 6:3), in which Noah built an ark and invited people to avail themselves of its protection, the judgment flood came and completely destroyed all mankind except the family of Noah. They had resisted the overwhelming evil of their time and became the progenators of a new humanity. But for a few exceptions, the biblical record does not give the story of the afflictions and tribulations of those fearful days. They could have learned the way of escape from Noah, who by faith, "being warned of God of things not seen as yet, moved with fear, prepared an ark to the saving of his house; by which he condemned the world, and became heir of the righteousness which is by faith" (Heb. 11:7).

Confusion of Men's Tongues at Babel

God's judgment upon mankind, resulting in the destruction of all but Noah's family, did not change the hearts even of Noah's descendants.

Perhaps a hundred years after the flood, when people had been divided into national groups, they manifested their worldly nature by attempting to make a name for themselves and built "a city and a tower whose top may reach unto heaven" (Gen. 11:4). If this tower was for protection from another possible flood, it showed disbelief in the promise of God that waters would never again destroy all flesh. Perhaps the real reason was the selfish desire to go their own way without God, choosing their course for themselves, as had their forefathers. God's judgment sent upon them was the confusion of their common language, making an unholy union with evil purpose difficult to accomplish (Gen. 11:8). As in every judgment, it is evident that God was demonstrating both His righteousness and His grace.

In this period of human history, we can see over and over tribulation as the weapon used by Satan to destroy souls and the instrument used by God to win souls back to Himself. It confirms the conclusion that tribulation is the universal experience of man in an unfriendly world where God's love can be satisfied with nothing less then a tested faith on the part of the ones who are to share His eternity with Him.

2

Tribulation and the Patriarchs

In order to understand that affliction, or tribulation, was a tool of a loving God in the development of a redemptive nation, it is necessary for us to consider the experiences of the ancestors of the children of Israel.

Over half of the Book of Genesis records the careers of Abraham, Isaac, and Jacob. The twelve sons of Jacob, except for Joseph, receive incidental notice. The biblical record clearly and candidly reveals the struggles of the patriarchs as they sought to match with faith the confidence the Lord God had placed in them.

ABRAHAM

One needs to be reminded of only a few of Abraham's troubles to understand that he suffered much in gaining his reputation as the friend of God and the father of the faithful.

First, there were the many difficulties in leaving old associates and traveling to an unknown land (Heb. 11:8). After some time famine came, causing Abraham to go to Egypt, only to be embarrassed by the king's abduction of Sarai, and by being royally rebuked for lying about her relationship to him. Still later Lot, Abraham's nephew, separated himself from his uncle and be-

came a resident of Sodom and was captured by a group of kings
that came against Sodom. This necessitated war on the part of
Abraham and his servants to rescue Lot, involving unrecorded
anxiety and suffering.

Then came the multiplied tribulations connected with God's
promise of a seed from Sarai to inherit the land. This tested
Abraham's faith severely, and led to much trouble. Sarai gave
her Egyptian maid to her husband, as they attempted to work
out the promise of God. Much sadness resulted: Hagar and her
son, Ishmael, were cast out and ultimately abandoned. In the
midst of their other troubles Sarai was abducted by Abimelech,
ruler of Gerar, but rescued by the Lord.

Despite Abraham's weakness of faith, Isaac was born. In light
of this, perhaps we can understand why it was necessary for the
Lord to test Abraham's faith by ordering him to offer up Isaac as
a sacrifice. Abraham's faith in God did not fail. For we read:

> By faith Abraham, being tried, offered up Isaac; yea, he that had
> gladly received the promises was offering up his only begotten
> son; even he to whom it was said, In Isaac shall thy seed be called:
> accounting that God was able to raise him up, even from the
> dead; from whence also he received him in a figure (Heb. 11:17–
> 19).

Does not the consideration of these trials of the one whom we
call the father of the faithful convince us that tribulation, when
met by a willing though weak faith, proves a blessing? Indeed,
Abraham's light affliction worked for him an exceeding and
eternal weight of glory.

ISAAC

Isaac, too, knew his trials. Who can understand his suffering
when about to be offered as a burnt offering by his father? He
afterward established a home ruled by favoritism on the part of
both husband and wife. Twins born in that home suffered from
deception and became enemies. Isaac was mistreated by the
Philistines who also abducted his wife. Esau chose a wife from

among the heathen. And blindness afflicted Isaac. In the midst of it all, "By faith Isaac blessed Jacob and Esau, even concerning things to come" (Heb. 11:20).

JACOB

Jacob, as he was introduced to the ruler of Egypt by his son, Joseph, summed up his life as a time of trouble: "The days of the years of my pilgrimage are an hundred and thirty years: few and evil have the days of the years of my life been, and have not attained unto the days of the years of the life of my fathers in the days of their pilgrimage" (Gen. 47:9). Jacob could have told of a mother who taught him to steal his brother's birthright by deception, resulting in the enmity of that brother and the grief of a blind father; of the deception of a father-in-law, resulting in plural marriages, with many difficulties following; of the abduction of a daughter and the revenge of her brothers in destroying the family of the abductor; of the grief caused by his sons' treachery in selling Joseph into slavery; and by being driven by famine into Egypt. But his faith was not destroyed, for Hebrews 11:21 tells us, "By faith Jacob, when he was dying, blessed each of the sons of Joseph; and worshipped, leaning upon the top of his staff."

JOSEPH

We should number Joseph among the patriarchs, even though the Seed of the Woman was not descended from his line. Certainly he played a very important part in the preservation of the redemptive nation. And he suffered much in preparation for his part. He was sold into slavery and separation from father and home, falsely charged with immorality by a conniving woman, forgotten by a released prisoner who had been befriended by him, and left to suffer unknown afflictions in prison. After two years the Lord jogged the memory of Joseph's fellow-prisoner, and Joseph was not only released, but because of his success in interpreting Pharaoh's prophetic dream, Pharaoh "made him ruler over all the land of Egypt" (Gen. 41:43). In this position he brought his father and brothers, with their families, to Egypt where under God they were molded into a unified nation. Joseph's faith was so strong in the covenant promise that God had made with Abraham, Isaac, and Jacob that he commanded that his bones be carried back to the Promised Land when they returned (Heb. 11:22). Approximately four hundred years later, when the children of Israel made their exodus from Egypt, "Moses took the bones of Joseph with him" (Exod. 13:19).

Joseph's career is an illustration, some say a type, of the career of Jesus: a favored son of his father, grossly mistreated by his brothers and others, but ultimately exalted to the place of ruler over all Egypt.

JOB

Any study of tribulation and God's people must include the Book of Job, which Jewish tradition attributes to the authorship of Moses. While Job was of the land of Uz, and, as far as we know, was not related to the biblical patriarchs, he belonged to that age. He was commended of the Lord as being "a perfect and an upright man, one that feareth God and escheweth evil" (Job 1:8). This Satan denied, suggesting that Job feared God because the Lord rewarded him for his goodness:

> Doth Job fear God for nought? Hast not thou made an hedge about him, and about his house, and about all that he hath on every side? Thou hast blessed the work of his hands, and his substance is increased in the land. But put forth thine hand now, and touch all that he hath, and he will curse thee to thy face (Job 1:9–11).

"And the Lord said unto Satan, Behold, all that he hath is in thy power; only upon himself put not forth thine hand" (Job 1:12). Later the Lord extended this permission to include "his bone and his flesh" (Job 2:5). Here again, as in the case of Adam, is introduced the mysterious actions of a God of love permitting the adversary to test the faith of Job. He intends to overrule that adversary and to perfect that faith.

Keeping these opposing purposes in mind, briefly recall the experience of Job. First, he was stripped of all his earthly possessions by Satan. Then his children were taken from him by a disastrous tornado. Next, he was afflicted by what the record describes as "sore boils from the sole of his foot unto his crown" (Job 2:7), which, in spite of the intense pain, may have caused Job less suffering than the advice of his wife: "Dost thou still retain thine integrity? Curse God, and die" (Job 2:9). There on the ash heap he sat, scratching at his sores and wondering, "Why?"

Finally, after the passing of several weeks, Eliphaz, the Temanite, and Bildad, the Shuhite, and Zophar, the Naamathite, came from their distant homes "to mourn with him and to comfort him" (Job 2:11).

But Job's three friends became miserable comforters. They had been his friends for a long time. Never before had there been any question about Job's integrity. But now, possessing only the world's explanation of human affliction and suffering, these friends became Job's tormentors. They charged him with sin. Eliphaz came to the point quickly:

> Remember, I pray thee, who ever perished, being innocent? Or where were the righteous cut off? Even as I have seen, they that plow iniquity, and sow wickedness, reap the same. By the blast of God they perish, and by the breath of His nostrils are they consumed (Job 4:7-9).

Adversity, suffering, and affliction were prima facia evidence to them of God's punishment for Job's sin. And the world of that day agreed with Eliphaz. The three friends prolonged their arguments to establish the false premise of the world's reasoning.

Indeed, Job himself had accepted this false reasoning. But he came to a point where he could not reconcile this false philosophy with his own experience of sincere devotion to his God. He could not accept the charge that he was being punished by the God whom he loved. There had to be some other reason for his tribulation. In the process of answering his accusers, Job gropes for the light, making many mistakes along the way. He never discovers the full truth until he comes face to face with his Maker. But now and again, a bit of truth flashes into his mind and heart.

Job begins to understand his distance from God. "He is not a man, as I am, that I should answer him, and we should come together in judgment. Neither is there any daysman betwixt us, that he might lay his hand upon us both" (Job 9:32–33). For one thing, Job's afflictions had worked for him in showing him the need of a go-between, or mediator. And soon after this Job could confidently say, "Though he slay me, yet will I trust in him" (Job 13:15).

Under the fire of his accusing friends the perplexity remains, but his experience is developing within him an uneasy confidence: "My witness [advocate] is in heaven" (Job 16:19). And he makes request of God, "Put me in a surety with thee" (Job 17:3). It is his affliction that is bringing about this better understanding that God Himself is his advocate and surety. And we are not surprised a little later to hear him cry out:

> Oh that my words were now written! Oh that they were printed in a book! That they were graven with an iron pen and lead in the rock for ever! For I know that my redeemer liveth, and that he shall stand at the latter day upon the earth: and though after my skin worms destroy this body, yet in my flesh shall I see God: whom I shall see for myself, and mine eyes shall behold, and not another; though my reins be consumed within me (Job 19:23–27).

And he later added, "He knoweth the way that I take, when he hath tried me, I shall come forth as gold" (Job 23:10).

His own ignorance, and that of his friends, impresses Job, and referring to some of his statements, he says:

> Lo, these are parts of his ways: but how little a portion is heard of him? But the thunder of his power who can understand?" (Job 26:14). "Whence then cometh wisdom? And where is the place of understanding? . . . God understandeth the way thereof, and he knoweth the place thereof. . . . And unto man he said, Behold, the fear of the Lord, that is wisdom; and to depart from evil is understanding (Job 28:20, 23, 28).

But Job longs for more wisdom and understanding, and cries out, just before the debate between himself and his friends comes to an end, "Oh that one would hear me! Behold, my desire is, that the Almighty would answer me, and that mine adversary had written a book. Surely I would take it upon my shoulder, and bind it as a crown to me" (Job 31:35–36). It was his cry for the written Word—the word from God which is our Bible.

Job had made progress in his devotion to God, but neither he nor his friends had found answers to their questions. At this point a new character, Elihu the Buzite, speaks. His words make the transition between the awful gap between Job's last words and Jehovah's appearance. He asks Job to recognize his own ignorance and to wait on God, the great teacher, for the truth. As Elihu closes his speech, from the whirlwind Jehovah challenges Job. He reveals His own greatness and power to Job, and, furthermore, He reveals Job's weakness to him. God challenges Job to measure his own wisdom and power by that of the Creator. When this is done, Job answers, "I have heard of thee by the hearing of the ear: but now mine eye seeth thee. Wherefore I abhor myself, and repent in dust and ashes" (Job 42:5–6).

It may surprise us that the many questions raised by Job and his friends do not receive direct and detailed answers from the Lord God. No theology of tribulation is unfolded. Rather, this revelation from God caused Job to see his own weakness and ignorance, and the privilege of rejoicing in a God of power and wisdom, the power of whom he cannot approach, the wisdom of whom he cannot begin to grasp. But he may rejoice in this wise and powerful God for His own sake. The infinite God wants a complete and unquestioning faith from man, like that of a child in his earthly father.

The result of the trial: "So the Lord blessed the latter end of Job more than his beginning" (Job 42:12).

This study of tribulation's way with the patriarchs, with its emphasis upon the fact that all whom the Lord loves He chastens, and that with great and eternal profit, should impress us with the importance of resisting the world's pressure even when it hurts. For those who resisted the chastening of the Lord fell into Satan's trap of self-deception and eternal ruin.

Will God's people of the latter days, whom we call the church, pass through great tribulation? How else can they be like God's ancient patriarchs of the faith?

3

Tribulation and the Redemptive Nation

The primitive history of the race revealed the necessity of the development of a special people to carry out the redemptive purpose of a loving God. So the Lord said to Abram:

> Get thee out of thy country, and from thy kindred, and from thy father's house, unto a land that I will shew thee: and I will make of thee a great nation, and I will bless thee, and make thy name great; and thou shalt be a blessing: and I will bless them that bless thee, and curse him that curseth thee: and in thee shall all families of the earth be blessed (Gen. 12:1–3).

The descendants of Abraham, then, would constitute a special people commissioned to prepare the way for the coming of the Seed of the Woman who would save men from sin. One might be tempted to think that the Lord, in developing this redemptive instrument, would protect it from all trials and troubles. Not so. Abraham's descendants found themselves as commissioned representatives of the true God in an unfriendly world under the influence of a powerful adversary, and, at the same time, the objects of God's forgiving love which would be poured out in death for them and for the rest of mankind. That meant that their earthly existence would be spent in the middle of a battlefield where two opposing powers were contending for the allegiance and devotion of man. Tribulation would become the constant experience of the Jewish nation, just as it is for all who are involved in bringing Christ to sinners.

THE EGYPTIAN AFFLICTION

In the process of making His covenant, the Lord said to Abraham, "Know of a surety that thy seed shall be strangers in a land that is not theirs, and shall serve them; and they shall afflict them four hundred years; . . . and afterward shall they come out with great substance" (Gen. 15:13–14). The Lord did not identify the nation that would enslave the children of Israel. And they did not know when they went into Egypt, under the protection of Joseph, that they would become Egypt's slaves.

But after an unknown number of years the influence of Joseph became ineffective, for

> There arose a new king over Egypt, who knew not Joseph. And he said unto his people, Behold, the people of the children of Israel are more and mightier than we: Come on, let us deal wisely with them . . . lest they join unto our enemies, and fight against us. . . . Therefore they did set over them taskmasters to afflict them with their burdens. . . . But the more they afflicted them, the more they multiplied and grew. . . . And the Egyptians made the children of Israel to serve with rigour; and they made their lives bitter with hard bondage, in mortar, and in brick, and in all manner of service in the field: all their service, wherein they made them serve, was with rigour (Exod. 1:8–14).

After the cruel king's death, the people cried out to God for relief, "And God heard their groaning, and God remembered his covenant with Abraham, with Isaac, and with Jacob. And God looked upon the children of Israel, and God had respect unto them" (Exod. 2:24–25).

The manner in which "God had respect unto them" is most instructive. First, He selected a leader to free His people from bondage by overruling Pharaoh's decree that every son born of the Hebrews be cast into the river, and by making one such child from the river not only the adopted son of the king's daughter, but the future savior of the Israelites with an education in Egyptian wisdom. And when this prince forty years later slew an Egyptian who was molesting an Israelite, he was forced to flee to the land of Midian, where he spent forty years learning the very wilderness in which he would lead and develop his people into a nation. Thus, by means of tribulation, the Lord prepared Moses for his great task, and at the same time endeared him to the hearts of his fellow Hebrews. Who dares suggest that the Lord might have found a better way to prepare a leader for His people?

Second, the Lord warned Moses, when He called him to his task, that it would not be an easy one. For, said the Lord, "I know that the king of Egypt will not give you leave to go, no, not by a mighty hand. And I will put forth my hand, and smite Egypt with all my wonders which I will do in the midst thereof: and after that he will let you go" (Exod. 3:19–20).

Ten plagues, devastating even to the first-born of the king, persuaded Pharaoh to let the people go. Too, they convinced the Israelites that the God of Moses was the true God of their fathers, and that the so-called gods of Egypt were false gods. By this means, and by nothing short of this means, were the children of Israel molded into a unity prepared for their journey into freedom.

THE WILDERNESS TRIALS

Only a little more than a year after the exodus, and after God had given the Israelites their laws, their tabernacle of meeting, their priesthood, and other institutions, they were ready to enter the Promised Land. But the people rebelled and threatened to elect a captain to lead them back to Egypt.

God's anger was aroused at so great a sin and He threatened to destroy the Israelites. Moses interceded. As punishment for their rebellion, God condemned them to forty years wandering in the wilderness, or until all over twenty years of age, with the exception of Joshua and Caleb, were dead. A plague devoured the leaders of the rebellion. Little is told of the suffering of the thirty-eight remaining years of wandering. The lesson of the importance of obedience to God was indelibly impressed upon their minds.

THE CANAANITE OPPOSITION

The three hundred years of the judges were the dark ages of Hebrew history. A cycle in four stages was constantly repeating itself in this period. First, the people sinned. Second, God sent an enemy nation to punish them. Third, the people prayed for deliverance. And fourth, God answered their prayers by raising up a deliverer to free them and to give them peace. Again, a loving Father was busy using the instrument of tribulation to whip them into line that they might become a great nation.

THE KINGDOM FAILURES

Finally the time came when the people insisted on having a king that they might be like the other nations round them. This was in effect a rejection of God as the ruler of the theocracy. But the Lord, like a loving parent, permitted it.

The United Kingdom

Saul, a young Benjaminite, was anointed by Samuel as the first king. Strong at first in his military exploits, Saul was not long in bringing upon himself the displeasure of the Lord by his disobedience. His jealousy of young David and other inconsistencies drove him to madness at times. Finally, in desperation Saul sought the help of the witch of Endor in bringing back Samuel from the grave to help him out of his troubles. But nothing helped. And he and his son, Jonathan, died in battle, and his throne was ultimately given to David, the son of Jesse, whom Samuel had secretly anointed.

David, limited to sovereignty over Judah and Benjamin for seven and a half years, while Ishbosheth, one of the remaining sons of Saul, attempted to hold on to Saul's kingdom in the north, finally gained control of the united nation. There was much of both prosperity and calamity in David's reign. His early wars solidified and extended the borders of the nation. But his double sin of adultery and murder brought many sorrows to David, his family, and his people. The Lord sent the prophet Nathan to him, rebuking him for his sin, and warning of trouble for his house and his kingdom (II Sam. 12:1–14). David sincerely repented of his sin and desired to build a temple for the Lord God. While he was denied this privilege, he gathered much material for its later building. The Lord entered into a covenant with David, promising that one descending from him would be a perfect king and would sit on his throne forever. This prophecy became the great hope of the people. And the memory of David was ever treasured in the hearts of the children of Israel.

Solomon, son of David, was the third ruler of the united kingdom, the first dynastic occupant of the throne. He may be described as the master sage, the iron ruler, the enterprising merchant, and the peaceful emperor. The borders of his kingdom reached the full extent of the land promised Abraham by the Lord, thus fulfilling God's promise. His reign was marked by extraordinary wisdom and inexcusable folly. He built a magnificent temple to the glory of the Lord God. He also built temples to the gods of his foreign-born wives. His erection of palaces, store cities, and fortresses, along with other luxuries, brought economic distress and slavery to his people.

> Marrying foreign wives was expedient politically, but not spiritually.... Foreign marriages brought foreign religions, and the king compromised the convictions which he had expressed in his dedicatory prayer for the temple (I Kings 8:23, 27) by engaging in syncretistic worship to placate his wives. This violent breach of Israel's covenant could not go unpunished. Though judgment was stayed during Solomon's lifetime for David's sake, the seed of dissatisfaction sown among the people by Solomon's harsh policies were to bear bitter fruit during the reign of his son Rehoboam.[1]

---

[1]D. A. Hubbard in *The New Bible Dictionary,* edited by J. D. Douglas (Grand Rapids: Eerdmans, 1962), p. 1204.

The Divided Kingdom

Rehoboam, the successor of Solomon, refused to take the advice of his older counselors to relieve the tax burden brought about by his father. This resulted in the division of the kingdom into a southern kingdom of the tribes of Judah and Benjamin under Rehoboam, and a northern kingdom of the ten remaining tribes, with Jeroboam I as the first king.

Northern kingdom of Israel and the Assyrian captivity

The doom of the northern kingdom was sealed at the very beginning when the first king, Jeroboam I, undertook to mix idolatry with the worship of the Lord God. He was followed by eighteen kings who almost succeeded in leading the people to forsake the Lord God entirely. The chief characteristic of each of Israel's kings, so emphatically noted in the sacred record, was that "he did evil in the sight of the Lord, and walked in the way of Jeroboam, and in the sin wherewith he make Israel to sin" (I Kings 15:34). In the slightly more than two hundred years of the northern kingdom's history (931–722 B.C.), nine separate dynasties were on the throne. Revolution, tyranny, heresy, apostasy, disintegration, murder, along with dependence on enemy nations, marked Israel's sad history. Two kings of the fifth dynasty, Joash and Jeroboam II, were able to bring the nation from virtual slavery to a degree of prosperity for a short period, but neither of these turned from the sin of Jeroboam I "wherewith he made Israel to sin." And within about thirty years of this short prosperity, Israel was conquered by Assyria and carried into captivity.

The cause of Israel's fall is clearly stated in II Kings 17:7–41; 18:12:

> For so it was, that the children of Israel had sinned against the Lord their God.... And had feared other gods, and walked in the statutes of the heathen, whom the Lord cast out from before the children of Israel.... Yet the Lord testified against Israel, and against Judah, by all the prophets, and by all the seers, saying, Turn ye from your evil ways, and keep my commandments and my statutes, according to all the law I commanded your fathers, and which I sent to you by my servants the prophets. Not-

withstanding they would not hear, but hardened their necks, like to the neck of their fathers, that did not believe in the Lord their God. . . . Therefore the Lord was very angry with Israel, and removed them out of his sight. . . . And the Lord rejected all the seed of Israel, and afflicted them, and delivered them into the hand of the spoilers, until he had cast them out of his sight. . . . So Israel was carried away out of their land to Assyria.

The experience of the northern kingdom of Israel is a classic example of how a righteous God used their afflictions as a terminal punishment for their sins when they refused to allow His loving discipline to mold them into a real part of the people who brought the Christ to men.

Southern kingdom of Judah and the Babylonian captivity

The southern kingdom of Judah (931–586 B.C.) continued for 134 years after the fall of the northern kingdom of Israel. The first reason for this was the Lord's protection and preservation of the dynasty of David, for He had determined that the Messiah should come from David's seed (II Sam. 7:12–17). Another reason was that three of Judah's God-fearing kings, Jehoshaphat, Hezekiah, and Josiah, led the people in revivals of devotion to the true God.

However, the history of Judah was that of continuous decline, three times arrested by the above mentioned kings, but finally ending in the fall and captivity in Babylon. Nebuchadnezzar destroyed the temple, breached the walls of Jerusalem, and took hostages of the chiefs of the people to Babylon. Only the poorest of the people were left in the land. Some of these fled to Egypt (II Kings 25:23–30), leaving the land desolate.

The cause of Judah's fall is given in II Chronicles 36:14–16:

All the chief of the priests, and the people, transgressed very much after all of the abominations of the heathen; and polluted the house of the Lord which he had hallowed in Jerusalem. And the Lord God of their fathers sent to them his messengers, rising up betimes, and sending; because he had compassion on his people, and on his dwelling place: but they mocked the messengers of God, and despised his words, and misused his prophets, until the wrath of the Lord arose against his people, till there was no remedy.

The Restored Remnant

Jeremiah had prophesied, "This whole land shall be a desolation, and an astonishment; and these nations shall serve the king of Babylon seventy years" (Jer. 25:11). Later the same prophet promised, "Thus saith the Lord, That after seventy years be accomplished at Babylon I will visit you, and perform my good word toward you, in causing you to return to this place" (Jer. 29:10).

The restoration of the sifted remnant of the people was a slow process. They returned in three groups. The first group, under Zerubbabel, went back about 535 B.C. The second group, under Ezra, went back about 458 B.C. And the third group, under Nehemiah, went back about 445 B.C. They dedicated their rebuilt temple about 516 B.C. But during the entire time of their return there was opposition from the Samaritans, and the Israelites were involved in immorality and religious practices contrary to the law of Moses. Ezra and Nehemiah succeeded in leading the people to enter into a solemn covenant to walk in the law of the Lord (Neh. 8–10). But the closing chapters of Nehemiah show that the remnant of Israel broke this covenant, as they had every other covenant between them and the Lord. Nevertheless, the Lord kept a small Jewish remnant dedicated to Him, in the land, and ultimately used that remnant in bringing the Messiah in flesh to the world. Many of the remnant accepted the Messiah, while many, especially the religious authorities, rejected Him and crucified Him. Their refusal to respond to Christ's saving appeal, left the nation without a mission. And their rejected king pronounced their doom: "Ye would not! Behold, your house is left unto you desolate" (Matt. 23:38). And Paul declared of these rejecting Jews, "The wrath is come upon them to the uttermost" (I Thess. 2:16). That wrath manifested itself in A.D. 70 in the destruction of the temple and the scattering of the people. And not one of the Old Testament prophets promised that the Lord would restore the Jews a third time to their land.[2]

---

[2]The first restoration was after the Exodus from Egypt. The second restoration was after the Babylonian captivity, to which Isaiah 11:11 refers.

Throughout the history of the redemptive nation, from the time of Moses and before, God was demonstrating His love for them, by sending His prophets to them, with warnings of danger and appeals for repentance. Besides the sixteen writing prophets, about thirty-eight others are known as prophets or seers. These were divinely inspired men, who spoke for God. Unlike the false prophets of other nations, these were the "holy · men of God who spake as they were moved by the Holy Ghost" (II Peter 1:21). They, too, suffered much in their service for the Lord.

A study of the experiences of Old Testament people shows us that tribulation is a common experience of mankind, teaching men to hate sin and love and obey the Lord. "Now all these things happened unto them for examples: and they are written for our admonition, upon whom the ends of the world are come" (I Cor. 10:11).

4

Daniel's Seventy Weeks

While Daniel 9:24–27 is primarily concerned with the first coming and saving work of the Messiah, it is by some made the basis for the teaching that there will be a seven year tribulation period before or near the time of the second coming of the Lord. Therefore, it is necessary for us to give this prophecy a place in our study.

THE CONTEXT

Daniel reports, "In the first year of his [Dairus's] reign I Daniel understood by the books the number of years, whereof the word of the Lord came to Jeremiah the prophet, that he would accomplish seventy years in the desolation of Jerusalem" (Dan. 9:2). Jeremiah had said, "For thus saith the Lord, That after seventy years be accomplished at Babylon I will visit you, and perform my good word toward you, in causing you to return to this place" (Jer. 29:10).

It seemed to Daniel that the time for the fulfillment of this prophecy was near. For he says:

> I set my face unto the Lord God, and said, O Lord, the great and dreadful God, . . . we have sinned, and have committed iniquity, and have done wickedly, and have rebelled even by departing

from thy precepts and from thy judgments. . . . O Lord, according
to all thy righteousness, I beseech thee, let thine anger and thy
fury be turned away from thy city Jerusalem, thy holy mountain:
because for our sins, and for the iniquities of our fathers,
Jerusalem and thy people are become a reproach to all that are
about us. Now therefore, O our God, hear the prayer of thy
servant, and his supplications, and cause thy face to shine upon
thy sanctuary that is desolate, for the Lord's sake. . . . O Lord,
hear; O Lord, forgive; O Lord, hearken and do; defer not, for
thine own sake, O my God: for thy city and thy people are called
by thy name (Dan. 9:3–19).

While he was still praying, Daniel tells us, the angel, Gabriel,
came to him, commissioned by the Lord to give him "skill and
understanding." Then follows the angel's revelation of the seventy weeks (Dan. 9:24–27): "Seventy weeks are determined
upon thy people and upon thy holy city . . . ," which we must
study with great care.

THE TIME

Gabriel reveals to Daniel that a definite block of time has been
determined, or *cut out*, in which to accomplish that which must
take place for the true restoration of God's people from bondage.

The Seventy Sevens

The context shows that these seventy weeks, as ordinarily
translated, could not be mere seven-day weeks. The majority of
interpreters agree that these weeks were weeks of years. However, the scholars tell us that the "sevens," or "weeks," are
really what they call *heptads*, or somewhat indefinite periods,
and that it may not be possible to measure this period with the
exactness that we apply to other historic periods. And it is
perhaps true that we cannot depend on the secular chronologies
of that time to help us with the exactness that some have
claimed. Allowing for this, the ordinary reader would surely
conclude that these approximately 490 years were continuous,
one following the other in the natural and literal order.

Terminus a quo

When was this period of seventy sevens to begin? The answer is in verse 25: "Know therefore and understand, that from the going forth of the command to restore and rebuild Jerusalem," this period begins.

If we are to interpret Scripture by Scripture, the *terminus a quo* was certainly the command of Cyrus, king of Persia. Isaiah, with amazing prophetic foresight, long before Gabriel's announcement, had reported the Lord as saying:

> I am the Lord . . . that saith to Jerusalem, Thou shalt be inhabited; and to the city of Judah, Ye shall be built, and I will raise up the decayed places thereof. . . . That saith to Cyrus, he is my shepherd, and shall perform all my pleasure: even saying to Jerusalem, Thou shalt be built; and to the temple, Thy foundation shall be laid. Thus saith the Lord to his anointed, to Cyrus, whose right hand I have holden, to subdue nations before him. . . . For Jacob my servant's sake, and Israel mine elect, I have even called thee by thy name: I have surnamed thee, though thou hast not known me (Isa. 44:24, 26, 28; 45:1, 4).

We should not be surprised, then, to find the account of Cyrus's proclamation that the children of Israel were to go up to Jerusalem to rebuild the city and the temple.

> Now in the first year of Cyrus king of Persia, that the word of the Lord spoken by the mouth of Jeremiah might be accomplished, the Lord stirred up the spirit of Cyrus king of Persia, that he made a proclamation throughout all his kingdom, and put it also in writing, saying, Thus saith Cyrus king of Persia, All the kingdoms of the earth hath the Lord God of heaven given me; and he hath charged me to build him a house in Jerusalem, which is in Judah. Who is there among you of all his people? The Lord his God be with him, and let him go up (II Chron. 36:22–23; see also Ezra 1:1–4).

Ignoring this "more sure word of prophecy" by Isaiah, and the positive record of its fulfillment by Ezra, dispensationalists date the seventy sevens from the decree of Artaxerxes made in 445 B.C., ninety or more years later than the decree of Cyrus, and after 50,000 Israelites had already returned from Babylon. They argue that Cyrus only commanded the people to rebuild the "house of the Lord," and not Jerusalem itself. But a careful reading of Isaiah 44:28 contradicts this argument: the Lord "saith of Cyrus, he is my shepherd, and shall perform all my pleasure: even saying to Jerusalem, Thou shalt be built; and to the temple, Thy foundation shall be laid."

Terminus ad quem

As to the *terminus ad quem* of this block of time, Daniel 9:24 gives the clear answer "Seventy sevens are determined upon thy people and upon thy holy city, to finish the transgression, and to make an end of sins, and to make reconciliation for iniquity, and to bring in everlasting righteousness, and to seal up the vision and prophecy, and to anoint the most Holy." Notice the five "ands" joining the six things described into one over-all purpose. This can only mean that the six things are to be accomplished within and not after the period of the seventy sevens. And all of these six things were accomplished once and for all when the Lord Jesus was crucified on the cross and rose from the dead. This is the only possible answer.

"The Time Is Fulfilled"

Jesus began His ministry announcing, "The time is fulfilled, and the kingdom of God is at hand: repent ye, and believe the gospel" (Mark 1:15). This remarkable statement has reference to the *terminus ad quem* of the seventy sevens of Daniel 9:24–27.

First, consider the two words the Lord used: *time* and *fulfilled*. *Time* in the Greek New Testament is *kairos*, and means "the fateful and decisive point," with strong, though not always explicit, emphasis on the fact that it is ordained by God. "The fact that this *kairos* is now present as God's gift in fulfillment of Old Testament prophecy is the first startling declaration of the primitive gospel of Jesus."[1] *Fulfilled, peplērōtai* in the Greek, means "to fill a specific measure up completely." Therefore Mark 1:15 speaks of "the *kairos* which, awaited by God's people

---

[1]Kittel, Gerhard *Theological Dictionary of the New Testament* (Grand Rapids: Eerdmans, 1965), Vol. III, pp. 459–60.

on the basis of the promise, has come with the appearance of
Jesus."[2]

Recall from the Introduction the quote by A. T. Robertson,
referring to the definite article: "In the Greek the article is associated with gesture and aids in pointing out like an index
finger." Jesus said, "*The* time" (*ho* kairos), using the definite
article. Doesn't this give us every right to insist that Jesus was
definitely referring to *the only time* in the Old Testament dating
His first appearing? On the authority of Jesus, therefore, we can
say that the seventieth week of Daniel is not future.

Is There a Gap Between the Sixty-ninth and Seventieth Seven?

One group of interpreters of Daniel's prediction insists that
there is a gap of centuries between the sixty-ninth and seventieth seven, thus justifying their belief in a seven-year tribulation just before or near the second coming of the Lord.

It is taught in the Scofield Reference Bible

> The proof that this final week has not yet been fulfilled is seen
> in the fact that Christ definitely relates its main events to His
> Second Coming (Mat. 24:6, 15). Hence, during the interim be-
> tween the sixty-ninth and seventieth weeks there must lie the
> whole period of the Church set forth in the N. T. but not revealed
> in the O. T. The interpretation which assigns the last of the sev-
> enty weeks to the end of the age is found in the Church Fathers.
> When this seventieth week was referred to during the first two
> and one-half centuries of the Christian Church, it was almost
> always assigned to the end of the age.[3]

We dare to challenge the statement that "Christ definitely
relates its [seventieth week's] main events to His Second Coming."

Jesus was not referring to His second coming in Matthew
24:6,15, but to His coming in judgment on Israel, declared when
He sent the Twelve on their preaching mission to the cities of

---

[2]Ibid., 1968. Vol. VI, p. 294.
[3]*New Scofield Reference Bible* (New York: Oxford University Press, 1967), p. 913.

Israel, "till the Son of man be come" (Matt. 10:23). Again, He said, "Verily I say unto you, There be some standing here, which shall not taste of death, till they see the Son of man coming in his kingdom" (Matt. 16:28; see also Mark 9:1; Luke 9:27). If language means anything, these comings of Christ, whatever they were, happened during the physical lifetime of His hearers. We have no right to ignore these words of Jesus and apply Matthew 24:6, 15 to His second appearing which is still future. We know that Christ's coming in judgment upon Israel did come within forty or so years. And we know that His kingdom came within that generation (Acts 2:29–36). See a fuller discussion of this in our chapter on "Christ's Olivet Prophecy," page 63.

"All these things" before Matthew 24:24; Mark 13:30; and Luke 21:32, which of course included Matthew 24:6, 15, had to take place long ago, for Jesus solemnly declared, "Verily I say unto you, This generation shall not pass away until all these things be accomplished."

Furthermore, the fact that some of the church fathers gave the Scofield interpretation does not make the interpretation correct. They made many mistaken interpretations, as history proves.

It is unreasonable

The gap theory is unreasonable.

Where periods of time are given beforehand in the prophecies of the Bible they always mean that the time-units composing the period named are continuous. This *must* be so, else the prediction would serve only to deceive those who believed it. We have *no other way* of describing and limiting a period of time than by stating the number of time units (hours, days, months, or years) contained therein. It is therefore *a necessary law of language* that the time-units *be understood as being connected together without a break.*

. . . Not only has God's measuring line been altered by the gap interpretation, but it has been changed from a line of *determined* length to one of *indeterminate* length. . . . A measure which has no *limits at all*, one which continues to enlarge its dimensions, which, from an original length of 490 years, has already been stretched to 2400, and is still elongating itself, is not a measuring line at all. It is an absurdity.[4]

It is not scriptural

We think we have already proved this point. But attempts are made to justify the gap theory by citing the following references: Psalm 22:23; 110:1–2; Isaiah 61:2; Daniel 2:31–45; 7:23–27; 8:24–25; 11:35–36; Hosea 3:4–5; 5:15; 6:1–2; I Peter 3:10–12.

While some of these so-called examples tell of successive events, not one of them gives a time measure of a series of events, and therefore do not qualify as proof-texts. Indeed, some of the references do not touch the subject at all.

How could serious Bible students offer such references to prove that time gaps are scriptural? Could they have mistakenly assumed the correctness of this view by seeing it stated in some book on prophecy? It is amazing how many interpretations are based on such unproved assumptions. Assumptions, or guesses, in biblical interpretation are dangerous; for, if you give a pure assumption the advantage of popular exponents and let it age gracefully while building itself into a tradition, for many it will become an axiom.

It is antichristian

We realize that to charge sincere Christians with being guilty of antichristian interpretations of the Word of God is a serious matter. But the charge can be documented with references from almost any of the writings of dispensationalists who deal with the prophecy of Daniel 9:24–27.

For instance, dispensationalists believe that the fulfillment of Daniel's prophecy, "to finish the transgression, and to make an end of sins, and to make reconciliation for iniquity, and to bring in everlasting righteousness" must be made in a time yet future for the Jews. In other words, what Christ did on Calvary did not accomplish these four things for the Jews—this, in spite of the

---

[4]Philip Mauro, *The Seventy Weeks* (Boston: Hamilton Brothers, 1923), pp. 95–96, 116–17.

fact that Daniel said this was the whole purpose of the seventy weeks.

Great efforts are made to explain these two different salvations. Some have said that the Jews will be saved "by sight" at the beginning of the great tribulation. Of course, that is not biblical. "For by grace are ye saved through faith; and that not of yourselves: it is the gift of God: not of works, lest any man should boast" (Eph. 2:8–9) was the only way Jew or Gentile could be saved according to Paul and the New Testament.

Furthermore, the gap-theorists tell us that the "he" of Daniel 9:27, who "shall confirm the covenant with many for one week, and in the midst of the week cause the sacrifice and oblation to cease" is not the Christ of Calvary, but a future Antichrist. We shall go into this more fully later. Here, however, we are saying that this interpretation, in the face of the proof of Christ's completion of the six things mentioned in verse twenty-four, substitutes a future Antichrist for the true Christ of the cross, "to confirm the covenant," the only covenant that could be or needed to be confirmed. If this is not antichristian, what is?

THE PEOPLE

"Seventy sevens are determined upon thy people and upon thy holy city." That was equivalent to saying "upon the Jews and upon Jerusalem." And, of course, they were the people directly involved in the prophecy. Edward J. Young is correct when he says, "It is true that the primary reference is to Israel after the flesh, and the historical Jerusalem, but since this very verse [24] describes the Messianic work, it also refers to the true people of God, those who will benefit because of the things herein described."[5]

But dispensationalists limit this reference to Daniel's people and Daniel's holy city, and insist that the six purposes (named in

---

[5]Edward J. Young, *The Prophecy of Daniel* (Grand Rapids: Eerdmans, 1949), p. 197.

verse 24) have not been fulfilled as far as the Jews are concerned but await fulfillment in the still future period of the millennium. This ignores, if it does not deny, the fact that Christ's death on the cross and resurrection from the grave "made an end of sins, and made reconciliation for iniquity, and brought in everlasting righteousness," for the Jew as well as the Gentile.

Daniel 9:24–27 must not be limited to the people of God of the Old Testament dispensation in isolation from the people of God of the New Testament dispensation. For our God has only one people whom "He chose in Christ before the foundation of the world . . . having predestinated us unto the adoption of children by Jesus Christ to himself, according to the good pleasure of his will" (Eph. 1:4–5). It is true that historically the people of God are divided into two groups: those making up the faithful Israelites *preparing* for the redemptive event, and those composed of believing Jews and Gentiles *fulfilling* the redemptive event. When the Redeemer came, He finished all that was necessary in the preparatory period by His death and his resurrection. Since Calvary, the purpose of God has been the process of fulfillment. Collectively both groups constitute one group, the "Israel of God" (Gal. 6:16).

Paul explains this new classification of the people of God to the Gentile church in Ephesus:

> Wherefore remember, that ye being in time past Gentiles in the flesh, who are called Uncircumcision by that which is called the Circumcision in the flesh made by hands; that at that time ye were without Christ, being aliens from the commonwealth of Israel, and strangers from the covenants of promise, having no hope, and without God in the world: but now in Christ Jesus ye who sometimes were far off are made nigh by the blood of Christ. For he is our peace, who hath made both one, and hath broken down the middle wall of partition between us, having abolished in his flesh, even the law of commandments contained in ordinances, for to make in himself of twain one new man, so making peace; and that he might reconcile both to God in one body by the cross, having slain the enmity thereby: and came and preached peace to you which were afar off, and to them that were nigh. For through him we both have access by one Spirit unto the Father (Eph. 2:11–18).

Galatians 3:28–29 designates believers in Christ as the heirs of promise, but it carefully reveals that racial, national, social, and physical distinctions are things of the past. "There is neither Jew nor Greek, there is neither bond nor free, there is neither male nor female; for ye are all one in Christ Jesus. And if ye be Christ's, then are ye Abraham's seed, and heirs according to the promise."

THE PURPOSE

Seventy weeks are determined . . . to finish the transgression, and to make an end of sins, and to make reconciliation for iniquity, and to bring in everlasting righteousness, and to seal up vision and prophecy, and to anoint the most Holy" (Dan. 9:24).

"To Finish the Transgression"

What is the meaning of *finish?* Some scholars say that it means "restrain"; others think it means "make complete." For two reasons it has to mean "make complete."

First, this passage has to do with the redemptive nation in the period when they were reaching the climax of their existence, the reason for their call as a peculiar people, namely, to present the Savior-Messiah to mankind.

Second, when this Savior-Messiah arrived and presented Himself to the nation, existing primarily for the one purpose of presenting this Savior-Messiah to the world, this nation nailed Him to a cross, crying out, "His blood be upon us and on our children" (Matt. 27:25). This transgression was not restrained. It advanced to the final state of deicide. Or as the New English Bible puts it, they "finished off what their fathers began."

How could their transgression be made more complete than by denial of the holy and just One, and their desire that a murderer be granted unto them, and by killing the Prince of Life? (Acts 3:14). In the plainest of words Paul declares that "the wrath is come upon them to the uttermost" (I Thess. 2:16). "To the uttermost" means, according to Arndt and Gingrich, "to the end, forever, through all eternity."

"To Make an End of Sins"

The second purpose of the set-apart time of seventy sevens was "to make an end of sins." Of the many scriptural references available only two are needed to establish who made an end of sins and the method by which He did it.

The first is the announcement of John the Baptist, pointing to Jesus, and saying, "Behold, the Lamb of God, which taketh away the sin of the world" (John 1:29). Jesus was the Person who made an end of sins and His sacrifice as the Lamb of God on the cross of Calvary was the method by which He did away with sins.

The second Scripture is Hebrews 9:26: "Now once in the end of the world hath he appeared to put away sin by the sacrifice of himself." Again the who and the how are clear. The Greek for *put away* means to abrogate, annul, declare invalid.

Here, let us make a clear distinction. Sins as such have reached their "end" in the atoning sacrifice of Jesus on the cross. That is in the past. But His sacrifice is effective only for the ones who accept redemption, put their trust in the Redeemer, and allow the Holy Spirit to direct their lives. Believers exercising obedient faith have the assurance that "there hath no temptation taken you but such as is common to man: but God is faithful, who will not suffer you to be tempted above that ye are able; but will with the temptation also make a way of escape, that ye may be able to bear it" (I Cor. 10:13). If you "submit yourselves therefore to God," you can "resist the devil," by obedient faith in the Savior, and the devil "will flee from you" (James 4:7). But if you continue in your sins, you must pay the penalty of rejecting the only One who can save you from eternal condemnation.

"To Make Reconciliation for Iniquity"

The third purpose of the period of seventy sevens was "to make reconciliation for iniquity." The Scriptures are clear:

God commendeth his love toward us, in that, while we were yet sinners, Christ died for us. Much more then, being now justified by his blood, we shall be saved from wrath through him. For if, when we were enemies, we were reconciled to God by the death of his Son, much more, being reconciled, we shall be saved by his life (Rom. 5:8–10).

For it pleased the Father that in him [Christ] should all fulness dwell; and, having made peace through the blood of his cross, by him to reconcile all things unto himself, by him, I say, whether they be things in earth, or things in heaven. And you, that were sometime alienated and enemies in your mind by wicked works, yet now hath he reconciled in the body of his flesh through death, to present you holy and unblameable and unreprovable in his sight (Col. 1:19–22).

"To Bring in Everlasting Righteousness"

The fourth purpose of the period of seventy sevens was "to bring in everlasting righteousness." God has made Christ Jesus our "wisdom, and *righteousness*, and sanctification, and redemption" (1 Cor. 1:30, italics mine). Everlasting righteousness is the *Person,* Jesus. Paul grieved over the people of Israel because they failed to see this truth. He said, "I bear them record that they have a zeal of God, but not according to knowledge. For they being ignorant of God's righteousness, and going about to establish their own righteousness, have not submitted themselves to the righteousness of God. For Christ is the end of the law for righteousness to every one that believeth" (Rom. 10:2–4).

These four purposes of the blocked off period of seventy sevens were, every one of them, accomplished when Jesus died on the cross and rose from the dead. Jesus said, after He had completed the cruel task of making an end of sin, and of making reconciliation for iniquity, and of bringing in everlasting righteousness, "It is finished" (John 19:30). As Jesus used that statement, according to the Greek New Testament, it has the meaning, "It stands finished and as a result is for ever done."

"To Seal Up the Vision and Prophecy"

The fifth purpose of the period of the seventy sevens was "to seal up the vision and prophecy." Edward J. Young gives a splendid explanation of the meaning:

Vision was a technical name for revelation given to Old Testament prophets (*cf.* Isa. 1:1, Amos 1:1, etc.). The *prophet* was the one through whom this vision was revealed to the people. The two words, vision and prophet, therefore, serve to designate the prophetic revelation of the Old Testament period. This revelation was of a temporary, preparatory, typical nature. It pointed forward to the coming of Him who was the great Prophet (Deut. 18:15). When Christ came, there was no further need of a prophetic revelation in the Old Testament sense.... When sin is brought to an end by the appearance of the Messiah, prophecy, which has predicted His coming and saving work, is no longer needed. It has fulfilled its task and is therefore sealed up.[6]

"To Anoint the Most Holy"

The meaning of the sixth purpose of the seventy sevens, "to anoint the most Holy," has puzzled the interpreters. Perhaps we can approach its meaning by recalling the Hebrew practice of anointing to the office of *prophet* (I Kings 19:16), to the office of *priest* (Exod. 28:41), and to the office of *king* (I Sam. 16:12–13). The anointing implied that the gifts of the Spirit, symbolized by the anointing oil, were imparted for the fulfillment of the duties of the particular office (Zech. 4; Isa. 61:1).

"Anointed" literally translates the name *Messiah* in the Hebrew, and the name *Christ* in the Greek. In the Lord Jesus, called the Christ, we have the fulfillment of the prophecies concerning the coming Prophet, Priest, and King.

In the original text "the most Holy" is literally "a most holy thing." But according to Dr. Oswald T. Allis, eminent Old Testament scholar:

The "anointing of a most Holy" may refer either to a person or a place. If to a person, the reference may be to the descent of the Holy Spirit on Jesus to fit Him for His Messianic work (Luke 3:22; 4:18); if to a place, it may refer to the entrance of the risen Christ into heaven itself, when through "His own blood He entered once for all into the holy place, having obtained redemption" (Heb. 9:12) for all the elect. In a word, we have in verse 24 the prophecy of the "satisfaction of Christ," of His obedience and

---

[6]Ibid., p. 200.

sufferings, by virtue of which the sinner obtains forgiveness and acceptance with God.[7]

THE DETAILS

Daniel 9:24, giving the six purposes to be accomplished during the period of seventy sevens, was, we repeat, complete and comprehensive, leaving no room for a separation and postponement of the seventieth seven from the other sixty-nine. In verses 25–27, the angel Gabriel follows this summation with details concerning the schedule of events.

Of Sixty-nine Weeks

"Know therefore and understand, that from the going forth of the command to restore and to build Jerusalem unto the Messiah the Prince shall be seven weeks, and threescore and two weeks: the street shall be built again, and the wall, even in troublous times" (Dan. 9:25).

When the angel gave this message to Daniel, the restoration of the Hebrews from Babylonian captivity had not begun. So the words "know and understand" were most significant. The beginning of the restoration would be when Cyrus gave the command that the people could return (Isa. 44:28). And the end of the sixty-nine weeks would mark the appearance of the Messiah. In the 483 years between those two dates, there would continue to be times of trouble, but the walls and streets of Jerusalem would be rebuilt. What an announcement it was! We are going back home! The Messiah is coming! The promise of God still holds in spite of the disobedience of the people that had to be punished by seventy years of exile in a strange land.

After Sixty-two Weeks

No detail is given concerning the first seven weeks. Presum-

---

[7]Oswald T. Allis, *Prophecy and the Church* (Philadelphia: Presbyterian and Reformed, 1945), pp. 113–14.

ably it was the period of resettlement and reorganization. And nothing more is given about the sixty-two weeks following the first week. After the first week and the sixty-two weeks, the dispensationalists wedge in hundreds of weeks, as we have seen. But Daniel reports nothing of the kind, and for a very good reason: nothing happened between the sixty-ninth and the seventieth weeks. Nothing ever happens between the sixty-ninth or seventieth of anything. The moment the sixty-ninth ends, the seventieth begins.

"And after threescore and two weeks," Gabriel predicts two dreadful things would happen: first, "Messiah shall be cut off, but not for himself" (Dan. 9:26). *Cut off* is used of the death penalty, and refers to a violent death. This gives us a clue as to how long after the sixty-ninth week this happened: this had to refer to the crucifixion, and that took place without any question "in the midst of the (seventieth) week" (Dan. 9:27). "But not for himself" seems to refer to the utter rejection of the Messiah both by God and by man. "We have no king but Caesar," cried the Jews. "My God, my God, why hast thou forsaken me?" were the words from the cross. In that hour of blackness He had nothing, nothing but the guilt of the sin of all those for whom He died. Utterly forsaken, He was cut off.

The second dreadful thing that would happen "after three-score and two weeks," would be the destruction of Jerusalem by a foreign prince. "And the people of the prince that shall come shall destroy the city and the sanctuary; and the end thereof shall be with a flood, and unto the end of the war desolations are determined" (Dan. 9:26b). The historic fulfillment of the prophecy in A.D. 70 when the Romans under Prince Titus destroyed the temple and the city, with a great overflowing, or flood of disaster, is the best interpretation of this prediction. This second disaster was not predicted for the seventieth week, but after the sixty-ninth without any indication of how long after. Actually it was about forty years, the full probationary period, according to the language of symbolism.

The first tragedy turned out to be the ending of sin when Jesus paid all of man's sin debt. The second finished the transgression of the redemptive nation.

"For One Week"

Now, Gabriel goes to the seventieth seven, in verse 27, and reveals the three great accomplishments of the last week: the confirmation of the covenant, the cessation of the sacrifice and the oblation, and the consummation of the desolate city.

The confirmation of the covenant

The "he" of verse 27 can only refer to the subject of the entire passage, the Messiah, the Prince (Dan. 9:24–27). To make it refer back to "the prince" of verse 26, where that prince is not even the subject of the sentence, imposes upon the passage a foreign personage who has not been introduced by the prophet. Besides, it takes the action away from the purpose of the seventy sevens, as set forth in verse 24, and makes it the action of an imaginary Antichrist who continues the transgression, prolongs sin, denies reconciliation for iniquity, and brings in seven years of unrighteousness. In other words it contradicts and nullifies the whole meaning of the prophecy. There is not a word in the text or the context to justify all this degradation of the Christ and the cross. Nor is there Scripture to justify this notion. The historical fulfillment of these seventy weeks is so clear and certain that no one can be wrong who says that they were fulfilled by the Lord Jesus Christ over nineteen hundred years ago. And there is no guess work or tricks in that interpretation.

Verse 27 begins, "And he shall confirm the covenant with many for one week." Gabriel did not say "He shall *make* a covenant." The Hebrew idiom to express such a thought is "to cut a covenant." Christ rather caused the covenant to prevail, to accomplish its purpose. By His obedience to the covenant conditions, and by His sacrificial death on the cross, He fulfilled the terms of the covenant made with Abraham and his seed, and converted that covenant into the everlasting covenant of His blood, shed "for *many* for the remission of sins" (Matt. 26:28, italics mine). "For one week" does not mean that the covenant was effective for only a week. It means that during the seventieth week of years, from His baptism to the empty tomb, or for three and a half years, He effectuated the covenant; then for the second half of that week He applied the effects of His atonement to men through His Holy Spirit-filled followers.

Cessation of the sacrifice and oblation

"And in the midst of the week He shall cause the sacrifice and the oblation to cease" (Dan. 9:27). This does not mean that the sacrifice and the oblation ceased for half of the seventieth week. They ceased forever as the result of the price of sin being paid in full, not by animal blood, but by the atoning blood of Jesus, the Lamb of God. And divine action said a symbolical, "Amen!" when "the veil of the temple was rent in twain from the top to the bottom" (Matt. 27:51). The entirety of worship by symbolic sacrifice was brought to an end by the one sufficient sacrifice of Calvary. To even think of this as the work of some future Antichrist is blasphemous.

The letter to the Hebrews goes into this whole matter. One reference from the passage states the fact adequately:

> This man, after he had offered one sacrifice for sins for ever, sat down on the right hand of God; from henceforth expecting till his enemies be made his footstool. Whereof the Holy Ghost also is a witness to us; for after that he had said before, This is the covenant that I will make with them after those days, saith the Lord, I will put my laws into their hearts, and in their minds will I write them; and their sins and iniquities will I remember no more. Now where remission of these is, there is no more offering for sin" (Heb. 10:12-18).

Consummation of the desolate city

Of the many and varying translations of the last parts of verses 26 and 27, we have adopted that of Edward J. Young: "And its end [is] with an overflow, and unto the end was [is] determined desolations" (v. 26). "And upon the wing of abominations [is] one making desolate, and until end and that determined shall pour upon the desolate."[8]

The subject of these words seems to be the final days or consummation of the sanctuary and the city, about which he has

---

[8]Young, pp. 206, 208.

just been speaking. Predetermined desolations will overflow the city and the sanctuary in the war brought by the Roman people and their prince until the very end of that war. "Thus, since the Messiah has caused sacrifice and oblation to cease, there comes a desolator over the Temple, and devastation continues until a full, determined end pours forth upon the desolation."[9]

This harmonizes with what the Lord Jesus said about the destruction of the temple:

> When ye therefore see the abomination of desolation, spoken of by Daniel the prophet, stand in the holy place, (whoso readeth, let him understand:) then let them which be in Judaea flee into the mountains. . . . For then shall be great tribulation, such as was not since the beginning of the world to this time, no, nor ever shall be" (Matt. 24:15, 21).

Then Jesus warned His hearers not to believe anyone saying that this was the second coming of Christ: "Believe it not. For there shall arise false Christs, and false prophets, and shew great signs and wonders; insomuch that, if it were possible, they shall deceive the very elect" (Matt. 24:23–24).

This explanation also fits what Jesus said just before His Olivet prediction: "Behold, your house is left unto you desolate" (Matt. 23:38). And this, it seems to us, infallibly fixes the seventieth seven of Daniel as fulfilled in the destruction of Jerusalem in A.D. 70. And it says absolutely nothing about a possible second fulfillment in the yet future in the nature of a seven-year tribulation just before or near His second appearing.

In this interpretation of Daniel's seventy weeks, we have rejected assumptions based on questionable systems of explanation. This has compelled us to consider the seventy sevens as a continuous and uninterrupted measure of time, for the reason that neither Scripture nor common sense justifies the interruption of a definitely measured period of time.

And we have rejected the notion that God's people must forever be two separate people: the Jewish kingdom and the church, with two different futures in the plan of God. Such a

---

[9]Ibid., p. 219.

notion overemphasizes the agent of redemption at the expense of its purpose, which was to bring a blessing to all the families of the earth, and to weld them, by the blood of the Redeemer, into one household of faith, "the Israel of God."

Finally, we have rejected the notion that Christ on the cross did not completely fulfill the six purposes of Daniel 9:24 for all mankind, whether Jew or Gentile. To limit our Savior's supreme redemptive work in the manner of dispensationalism puts the only institution He ever established, the church, on a side track merely "to call out a people for his name," while reserving the great missionary task of winning most lost souls for a people that crucified Him and has until this day refused as a people to have Him in their lives.

5

Christ's Olivet Prophecy

Without doubt the greatest prophet ever to make a prediction was the Lord Jesus Christ. He alone could claim, "I myself am the truth" (John 14:6). God "hath in these last days spoken unto us by his Son" (Heb. 1:2). He is the Word or communication of God made flesh (John 1:1, 14).

He is *the* prophet of whom Moses spoke: "The Lord thy God will raise up unto thee a prophet from the midst of thee, of thy brethren, like unto me; unto him ye shall hearken" (Deut. 18:15). Heaven's messenger told John, the revelator, "The truth revealed by Jesus is the inspiration of all prophecy" (Rev. 19:10, Weymouth). And Paul is positive: "For all the promises of God in him are yea, and in him Amen, unto the glory of God by us." (II Cor. 1:20).

Let us see what this greatest of all prophets said about the future tribulation of His people and His future coming when He spoke to His disciples from the Mount of Olives, being careful neither to add to or take from His words, as found in Matthew 24, Mark 13, and Luke 21.

THE CONTEXT

After the hard climb from Jericho and a quiet Sabbath in the village of Bethany, Jesus and His disciples made their way to the city of Jerusalem and the temple. At His direction, the disciples had secured a colt from a nearby village and had set Jesus thereon in what may have seemed to them preparation for His public assertion of royalty. But

how different the vision of the future in their minds and His! They dreamed of a throne; He knew it was a Cross. Round the southern shoulder of Olivet they came, and, as the long line of the Temple walls burst on the view, and their approach could be seen from the city, they broke into loud hosannahs, summoning, as it were, Jerusalem to welcome its King.[1]

The Lamenting King

We see the sorrowing King plunged in bitter grief in the very hour of His triumph. Who can venture to speak of that infinitely pathetic scene? The fair city, smiling across the glen, brings before His vision the awful contrast of its lying compassed by armies and in ruins. He hears not the acclamations of the crowd. "He wept," or, rather, "wailed,"—for the word does not imply tears so much as cries.[2]

Luke alone tells us that as He was entering the city, Jesus cried out,

If thou hadst known, even thou, at least in this thy day, the things which belong to thy peace! But now they are hid from thine eyes. For the days shall come upon thee, that thine enemies shall cast a trench about thee, and compass thee round, and keep thee in on every side, and shall lay thee even with the ground, and thy children within thee; and they shall not leave in thee one stone upon another; because thou knowest not the time of thy visitation (Luke 19:42–45).

It was a painful preview of the prophecy of judgment He would two days later unfold to His disciples on the Mount of Olives.

"Behold, Your House Is Left Unto You Desolate."

On Monday morning "Jesus went into the temple of God" and cleansed it of its "den of thieves." Then He taught the eager

---

[1]Alexander Maclaren, *Gospel of Luke,* p. 185.
[2]Ibid., p. 187.

people, and enraged the chiefs of the people (Luke 19:47–48). Tuesday was a day of controversy, when the rulers challenged His authority and sought to "entangle him in his talk." Not only did He silence them, but He launched seven woes, like seven thunderbolts against them. It was the wailing of an infinite compassion, rather than the accents of anger; and it alone is heard in the outburst of lamenting in which Christ's heart runs over, as in a passion of tears, He cries:

> O Jerusalem, Jerusalem, thou that killest the prophets, and stonest them which are sent unto thee, how often would I have gathered thy children together, even as a hen gathereth her chickens under her wings, and ye would not! Behold, your house is left unto you desolate (Matt. 23:37–38).

THE DISCIPLES' QUESTION

As Jesus and His disciples departed from the temple that Tuesday afternoon, you can be sure that the disciples' minds were confused by what they had heard, especially that last word, "Your house is left unto you desolate." Did He mean that their temple would be abandoned?

The Jews were justly proud of their magnificent temple. It symbolized the presence of the true God with His people. It was, with its symbolic ceremonies, the very heart of the nation. With what He had said about its desolation fresh in their minds, Jesus' disciples called His attention to the temple buildings as they passed by (Matt. 24:1).

"And Jesus said unto them, See ye not all these things? Verily I say unto you, there shall not be left here one stone upon another, that shall not be thrown down" (Matt. 24:2). They had not misunderstood. He *did* mean that their temple would be destroyed. So, when they reached the Mount of Olives, "Peter and James and John and Andrew asked him privately, Tell us, when shall these things be? and what shall be the sign of thy coming, and of the end of the world?" (Matt. 24:3).

> What did they mean by "these things," by "Thy coming," by "the consummation of the age"? One cannot believe that these men meant: When shall be Thy second advent?... The second

advent must be prepared for fundamentally by the Cross and the Resurrection; and they had no apprehension of the Resurrection. He had told them again and again that He must suffer, and that He would rise again, but they had never grasped the truth of the Resurrection, or consented to the necessity of the Cross. They were in revolt against the idea of the Cross, and blind to the fact of the Resurrection. So that if we take this question not in the way our Lord answered it, but in the way they asked it, we see that they thought that presently, in some way or other He would pass out of sight, perhaps would escape from this pronounced hostility of the rulers. And yet they had heard Him say, that the very scene before them was to be one of devastation and desolation; and they said, "Tell us, when shall these things be? and what shall be the sign of Thy coming, and of the consummation of the age?" If these things are to be, if this Temple is to be destroyed, if Thou art coming in judgment? when art Thou coming in judgment? Their question simply meant, When art Thou going to do these things? . . .

They thought of these things as closely connected. One of the first things that we discover in the reading of the prophecy which followed is that Christ corrected the false impression. They said, "These things . . . the sign of Thy presence . . . and of the end of the age." He spoke of "these things," that is, the destruction of Jerusalem, which He had foretold; and then of the coming of the Son of Man, and of the consummation. . . . He separated His coming from "these things." . . . It may be said that there are other senses in which He was spiritually present at the destruction of Jerusalem, and there is no doubt that that is so. Nevertheless, He separated His coming at the end of the age from the destruction of Jerusalem with great care, rather than associated it therewith.[3]

THE DIVISION OF THE PROPHECY

The confused interpretations of the Lord's Olivet prophecy are largely due, as Dr. Morgan has indicated, to the failure to distinguish between the coming of the Lord in judgment upon Israel and His second appearing. The Lord offered definite

---

[3]G. Campbell Morgan, *The Gospel According to Matthew* (New York: Revell, 1929), pp. 282–83.

safeguards against such confusion in His answer to the disciples' question. In the time text (Matt. 24:34; Mark 13:30; Luke 21:32) Jesus distinguished between the time of the judgment of Israel and the time of His second appearing. And the transition text (Matt. 24:36; Mark 13:32) indicates the point where He turns from His prophecy of the destruction of Jerusalem to the facts regarding the last day, or the day of His appearing.

The Time Text

"Verily I say unto you, this generation shall not pass, till all these things be fulfilled." "All these things" were the things He had prophesied from the beginning of the discourse to this point. To the plain statement He adds a pledge, "Heaven and earth shall pass away, but my words shall not pass away" (Matt. 24:35; Mark 13:31).

The Scofield Reference Bible challenges this simple statement of our Lord:

> The word "generation" (Gr. *genea*), though commonly used in Scripture of those living at one time, could not mean those who were alive at the time of Christ, as none of "these things"—*i.e.*, the world-wide preaching of the kingdom, the tribulation, the return of the Lord in visible glory, and the regathering of the elect— occurred then. The expression "this generation" here ... may be used in the sense of *race* or *family*, meaning that the nation or family of Israel will be preserved "till all these things be fulfilled," a promise wonderfully fulfilled to this day.[4]

Note the four things Scofield said could not have occurred in that generation: First, "the world-wide preaching of the kingdom." Paul, however, told the Colossians, "The gospel, which ye have heard ... was preached to every creature which is under heaven" (Col. 1:23). And he was pleased that the faith of the Romans was "spoken of throughout the whole world" (Rom. 1:8).

Second, Dr. Scofield said that "the tribulation" could not

---

[4]Scofield Reference Bible (New York: Oxford University Press. 1967), p. 1035.

have occurred in that generation. Josephus, the Jewish historian, in reporting the destruction of Jerusalem in A.D. 70, said, "No city ever endured similar calamities, and no generation ever existed more prolific in crime."

Third, Dr. Scofield said that "the return of the Lord in visible glory" could not have occurred in that generation. No, that generation did not witness the second appearing of the Lord, but it did "see the Son of man coming in the clouds of heaven with power and great glory" in judgment upon Israel, and "coming in his kingdom" (Matt. 16:28), as we shall explain more fully later in this study.

Fourth, Dr. Scofield said that "the regathering of the elect" could not have occurred in that generation. Jesus did not say that there would be a *re*gathering of the Jews, as Dr. Scofield seems to imply. He said that His messengers (angels) would "gather together His elect from the four winds" (Matt. 24:31), not regather the Jews to Palestine. And this gathering of the elect has been happening ever since the Lord gave the great commission and sent His followers out to make disciples of all the nations.

According to Young's *Concordance*, not once did Jesus use the word *genea* for *race* or *nation* or *family*. Every time He used the word He meant those living at that time. Therefore, we are following Jesus as our interpreter, when we say that everything in Matthew 24:3–35, Mark 13:3–31, and Luke 21:7–33 would take place while many of His listeners were still alive in the flesh. This guideline may force us to revise our ideas, but the abandonment of our misunderstandings for His truth can only be a blessing.

The Transitional Test

The Lord clearly turned from a prediction concerning the fall of Jerusalem to things concerning the final day of His second appearing when He said, "But of that day and hour knoweth no man" (Matt. 24:36). In the Greek *"the* day, *that* one" has both the demonstrative pronoun (*ekainos*) and the definite article, which sets it apart as the particular day, a day of special significance above other days. Therefore, what follows Matthew 24:35 has to do with the future, while what He has said before that verse is past history.

We shall find that the Lord is definite about many things in the first section of His prophecy. There will be definite signs of the immediate destruction of Jerusalem and the temple. But in complete contrast, the time of His second appearing will be unknown, life will be going on as usual, and the final judgment will find the multitudes unready.

The first section of our Lord's prophecy is limited to Jerusalem, and the temple in particular. There is no hint of a rebuilt Jerusalem or temple. Rather, "There shall not be left one stone upon another that shall not be thrown down" (Matt. 24:2). In the second section there is no mention of a pre-tribulation or a post-tribulation coming of the Lord, nor of a seven-year tribulation, nor of a millennium.

These guidelines must be carefully observed, for they are on the authority of the supreme Prophet. We should not think of altering His predictions or putting words into His mouth.

THE WARNING ABOUT SIGNS

"What shall be the sign of thy coming?" How often we have heard sermons on the signs of Christ's coming, using the very signs that our Lord warned against as the basis of these sermons. We forget that Jesus condemned all sign seeking (Matt. 12:39–40). "Take heed that no man deceive you" (Matt. 24:4), He warned, mentioning five false signs.

Pretenders

"Many shall come in my name, saying, I myself [emphatic *egō*] am Christ; and shall deceive many" (Matt. 24:4–5; see also Mark 13:5–6; Luke 21:8). "To deceive" here means to trick one into believing what is not true. This is Christ's first, but not His last, warning against confusing the destruction of Jerusalem with His second appearing.

Ordinary Occurrences

> And ye shall hear of wars and rumours of wars: see that ye be not troubled: for all these things must come to pass, but the end is not yet. For nation shall rise against nation, and kingdom against kingdom: and there shall be famines, and pestilences, and earthquakes, in divers places. All these are the beginning of sorrows (Matt. 24:6-8; see also Mark 13:7-8; Luke 21:9-11).

Luke adds, "Fearful sights and great signs shall there be from heaven."

Such common occurrences are never to be taken as indications that the second appearing, or the end of the world, is at hand. These are things that have always been and will always be as long as the world stands.

Persecution

"Then shall they deliver you up to be afflicted, and shall kill you: and ye shall be hated of all nations for my name's sake. And then shall many be offended, and shall betray one another, and shall hate one another" (Matt. 24:9-10; see also Mark 13:9, 11-13; Luke 21:12-19). Mark and Luke add that the persecuted Christian will be defended by the Holy Spirit, and should endure faithfully to the end.

"Then" at the beginning of the above reference does not mean "thereafter," but at the time of the beginning of sorrows. "To deliver up" refers to being delivered to tribunals, courts, and even mobs, as in the case of Paul. "To be afflicted" is from the verb for "tribulation" in the Greek. It refers to the constant pressure that attends the Christian life, and has no direct reference to "a great tribulation."

False Prophets

"And many false prophets shall rise, and shall deceive many" (Matt. 24:11, Mark 13:10). Peter (II Peter 2:1-2), John (I John 4:4), and Paul (Acts 20:29-30) echoed this prophecy of the Lord, but neither of these suggested that this was a sign of the soon coming of the Christ. Josephus confirms the prophecy of Jesus concerning the presence of false prophets at the time of the destruction of Jerusalem in A.D. 70 (*Wars of the Jews*, VI.V).

Transgressions

"And because iniquity shall abound, the love of many shall wax cold. But he that shall endure unto the end, the same shall be saved" (Matt. 24:12–13).

Many interpreters consider this a prime sign of the soon coming of Christ. They forget that Jesus at the beginning of this list said, "Take heed that no man deceive you" (Matt. 24:4), then follows the list of deceptions, of which transgression is one. Our Lord was not describing either apostasy or perseverance as a sign of His soon return.

THE END OF THE JEWISH AGE

The Lord was surprisingly definite about the time of the end of the Jewish age. He clearly indicated what would happen before the end, at the end, and after the end. And He dated the time of the end by linking it with Daniel's measured history of the Jewish nation.

Before the End

As we have noted above, Jesus warned the disciples not to be deceived by the presence of pretenders, other ordinary occurrences, persecution, false prophets, and transgressions. But He added, "These things must come to pass, but the end is not yet" (Matt. 24:6; Mark 13:7; Luke 21:9). After naming these things, He says, "These things are the beginning of sorrows" (Matt. 24:8; Mark 13:8).

At the End

Three things will mark the end of the Jewish age: First, "This gospel of the kingdom shall be preached in all the world for a witness unto all nations, and then shall the end come" (Matt.

24:14). The Greek word for "end" (*telos*) means the "last part, close, conclusion." Sometime in the A.D. 60s, Paul wrote to the Colossian church, declaring that the gospel had been "preached to every creature which is under heaven" (Col. 1:23). Thus the gospel reached the ends of the earth just a short time before Jerusalem reached the end of its Jewish history. Tradition lends its support to Paul's testimony when it says that Andrew preached the gospel in Scythia, Philip in Phrygia, Bartholomew in India, Matthew in foreign lands, James Alphaeus in Egypt, Thaddaeus in Persia, Simon Zelotes in Egypt and Britain, and John Mark in Alexandria.

Second, "When ye therefore shall see the abomination of desolation, spoken of by Daniel the prophet, stand in the holy place, (whoso readeth, let him understand:) then let them which be in Judaea flee into the mountains . . . " (Matt. 24:15–16). Jesus didn't explain these words, unless Luke 21:20, 22 gives His clarification of His words: "When ye shall see Jerusalem compassed with armies, then know that the desolation is nigh. . . . For these be the days of vengeance, that all things which are written may be fulfilled."

There can be little doubt that our Lord was referring to Daniel 9:26, 27: "The people of the prince that shall come shall destroy the city and the sanctuary; and the end thereof shall be with a flood, and unto the end of the war desolations are determined. . . . And for the overspreading of abominations he shall make it desolate, even unto the consummation." In A.D. 70, the Roman army, carrying its military standard, with its eagle of silver or bronze, and under that an imperial bust which the soldiers were accustomed to worship, would be an abomination to devout Jews, for it would break the second commandment standing anywhere in the holy city.

The Lord certainly expected some of His disciples to be alive when the abomination stood in the holy place, for He urged them to flee to the mountains with great haste (Matt. 24:15–20; Mark 13:14–18) and with much prayer. Eusebius reports that many Christians heeded the warning and escaped.

Third, "For then shall be great tribulation, such as was not since the beginning of the world to this time, no, nor ever shall be. And except those days should be shortened, there should no flesh be saved: but for the elect's sake those days shall be short-ened" (Matt. 24:21–22; see also Mark 13:19–20). Luke 21:23–24 adds: "For there shall be great distress upon the land, and wrath unto this people. And they shall fall by the edge of the sword, and shall be led captive into all nations: and Jerusalem shall be trodden down of the Gentiles, until the time of the Gentiles be fulfilled."

We are insisting that this "great tribulation" was completely and finally fulfilled in the destruction of Jerusalem in A.D. 70. To resort to the so-called law of double reference, which we have shown above to be a violation of the principle of correct interpre-tation, and to insist that there is yet a future fulfillment to come in connection with our Lord's second appearing, is to abandon literalism and introduce confusion into the understanding of God's Word.

Did the fall of Jerusalem in A.D. 70 fulfill the Lord's prediction?

> It must be emphasized that the terribleness of the seige of Jerusalem was augmented by the suffering and horror which the Jews inflicted upon each other. Three vicious factions fought for the control of the city. Each group robbed, tortured, and slaughtered the others who refused to join its own faction. Many of the crimes committed within the city are unmentionable. Aged men and women suffered so much from the internal war that they longed for the Romans to come to deliver them from their domestic enemies. Although there was plenty of food to support the people in a seige for years, these factions by their evil passions set on fire those houses that were full of corn and other provisions. Not even the Temple was spared but was used as a battle-ground by these warring parties. Worshippers were killed before the altar and hundreds of the dead were strewn within the Temple.[5]

The Lord warned His disciples not to misunderstand His prophecy, saying,

> Then [at the time of great tribulation] if any man shall say unto you, Lo, here is Christ, or there; *believe it not*. For there shall arise

---

[5]J. Marcellus Kik, *An Eschatology of Victory* (Nutley, NJ: Presbyterian and Re-formed, 1971), p. 117.

> false Christs, and false prophets, and shall shew great signs and
> wonders; insomuch that, if it were possible, they shall deceive
> the very elect. . . . Wherefore if they shall say unto you, Behold,
> he is in the desert; go not forth: behold, he is in the secret chambers;
> *believe it not.* For as the lightning cometh out of the east, and shineth
> even unto the west; so shall also the coming [*parousia*] of the Son
> of man be. For wheresoever the carcase is, there will the eagles
> be gathered together (Matt. 24:23–28; see also Mark 13:21–23,
> italics mine).

We must not miss the significance of our Lord's words. He
instructed His disciples to refuse to believe anyone reporting
His visible presence during the tribulation experience. Further,
He indicated that His parousia would be no more secret than the
lightning flash. His coming in final appearance will be plainly
visible to all. Just as the eagles are instinctly aware of carrion and
gather to devour it, His parousia cannot be secret. Everybody
will see it. This was the explanation of the greatest of all
prophets, who was the embodiment of all truth. How could He
make the fact that His second appearing was in no way connected with the tribulation of the Jews any clearer?

After the End

"Immediately"

"Immediately after the tribulation of those days shall the sun
be darkened, and the moon shall not give her light, and the stars
shall fall from heaven, and the powers of the heavens shall be
shaken" (Matt. 24:29; see also Mark 13:24–25). Luke's report
says:

> And there shall be signs in the sun, and in the moon, and in the
> stars; and upon the earth distress of nations, with perplexity, the
> sea and the waves roaring; men's hearts failing them for fear, and
> looking after those things which are coming on the earth: for the
> powers of heaven shall be shaken (Luke 21:25–26).

"Immediately after the tribulation of those days" leaves no
room for a long interval of hundreds of years. What Jesus is
about to predict shall happen *at once.* Therefore, the darkened

sun, the lightless moon, and the falling stars cannot describe the "collapse of the whole siderial world," as some commentators say, for history proves that nothing like that happened immediately after the fall of Jerusalem. Too, what Jesus said about "all these things" happening in that generation forces us to confine our interpretation to things taking place soon after the fall of Jerusalem.

The Old Testament prophets often described the fall of nations in the same terms used by Jesus in this prophecy. Isaiah, for instance, warned Babylon,

> The day of the Lord is at hand; it shall come as a destruction from the Almighty. . . . For the stars of heaven and the constellations thereof shall not give their light: and the sun shall be darkened in his going forth, and the moon shall not cause her light to shine. And I will punish the world for their evil, and the wicked for their iniquity; and I will cause the arrogancy of the proud to cease, and will lay low the haughtiness of the terrible (Isa. 13:6, 10–11).

He uses the figures of Israel:

> It shall come to pass in that day, that the Lord shall punish the host of the high ones that are on high, and the kings of the earth upon the earth. . . . Then the moon shall be confounded, and the sun ashamed, when the Lord of hosts shall reign in Mount Zion, and in Jerusalem, and before His ancients gloriously (Isa. 24:21, 23).

Ezekiel, speaking of the destruction of Egypt, writes:

> When I shall put thee out, I will cover the heaven, and make the stars thereof dark; I will cover the sun with a cloud, and the moon shall not give her light. All the bright lights of heaven will I make dark over thee, and set darkness upon thy land, saith the Lord God (Ezek. 32:7–8).

Other prophets used similar language in describing the fall of nations (Dan. 8:10; Joel 2:10, 30, 31; Amos 8:9–10). In figurative language, they made the heavenly bodies emblems of human governments. See also Hebrews 12:25–27 and Revelation 6:12–17.

"And then"

> "And then [at that time] shall appear the sign of the Son of man in heaven: and then [at that time] shall all the tribes of the earth mourn, and they shall see the Son of man coming in the clouds of heaven with power and great glory. And he shall send his angels with a great trumpet, and they shall gather together his elect from the four winds, from one end of heaven to the other" (Matt. 24:30–31; see also Mark 13:26–27; Luke 21:27).

And Luke 21:28 adds, "But when these things begin to come to pass, look up, and lift up your heads; for your redemption draweth nigh." From this added word of Luke it is evident that some of the disciples would still be alive when these things happened. "These things" according to this word of Luke, could not be centuries after the fall of Jerusalem. They were taking place at the same time. A careful study of "these things" will prove this statement to be true.

First, "the sign of the Son of man in heaven shall appear." What was this "sign of the Son of man"? It had to be something extraordinary that would authenticate the person and work of Jesus as the Messiah. The Jews had asked Him for such a sign. Twice He had answered them, "An evil and adulterous generation seeketh after a sign; and there shall no sign be given it, but the sign of the prophet Jonas" (Matt. 12:39; see also 16:4). Once He answered when asked for such a sign, "Destroy this temple, and in three days I will raise it up. . . . He spake of the temple of His body" (John 2:19, 21). Twice

> to those who ask for a sign Jesus replies with a riddle. The sign of Jonah will be renewed with the manifestation of the Son of man returning from the dead. This is the only sign which will be given them. . . . As Jonah became a sign to the Ninevites, obviously as one who had been delivered from the belly of the fish, Jesus will be displayed to this generation as the One who is raised up from the dead. . . . Both the old and the new sign of Jonah consist in the authorization of the divine messenger by deliverance from death.[6]

---

[6]Joachim Jeremias in *Theological Dictionary of the New Testament, edited by Gerhard Kittel (Grand Rapids: Eerdmans, 1964), pp. 409, 410.*

The apostle Paul definitely verifies this interpretation: "Concerning His Son Jesus Christ our Lord, ... declared to be the Son of God with power, according to the spirit of holiness, by the resurrection from the dead" (Rom. 1:3–4).

Second, coupled with this appearance of the sign of the Son of man in heaven, the coming of the Son of man on the clouds in judgment upon Israel will be experienced. This cannot be the second appearing of the Lord, for He Himself had clearly indicated (Matt. 24:23–28) that His second coming would not be in connection with the destruction of the temple. And again the Lord looks back on all these things and declares, "Verily I say unto you, This generation shall not pass, till all these things be fulfilled" (Matt. 24:34). This testimony of Jesus compels us to see this coming of the Lord in judgment upon Israel as a fulfillment of His previous prophecy: "Verily I say unto you, There be some standing here, who shall not taste of death, till they see the Son of man coming in his kingdom" (Matt. 16:28).

Here we have two consequences of the destruction of the temple: the dissolution of the Jewish nation, and the resurrected Son of man reigning over the kingdom of God in heaven. The desolation of the temple, representing the redemptive nation raised up to bring salvation to the world, was evidence that the chosen nation had failed to accept the blessing intended for it, and now goes down in judgment for that failure. But, in spite of the nation's failure, God, by means of a remnant of that nation, succeeds in bringing the victorious Messiah through death and resurrection to a never ending life on the throne of heaven. The dissolution of the temple brought grief to the rejecting Jews. The resurrection and victory of the eternal King brings joy to those who trust Him.

In this prophecy, our Lord is seeing the fulfillment of Daniel's prediction:

> I saw in the night visions, and, behold, one like the Son of man came with the clouds of heaven, and came to the Ancient of days, and they brought him near before him. And there was given him dominion, and glory, and a kingdom, that all people, nations, and languages, should serve him; his dominion is an everlasting dominion, which shall not pass away, and his kingdom that which shall not be destroyed (Dan. 7:13–14).

The risen Christ announced His victory in Galilee: "All power is given unto me in heaven and in earth" (Matt. 28:18). His triumph at the cross spoiled principalities and powers (Col. 2:15). And "when He ascended up on high, He led captivity captive" (Eph. 4:8). The apostle John, in Revelation 5, gives a marvelous description of the risen Christ taking His throne and authority.

The destruction of the temple brought to an end the offering of animal sacrifices. The sin debt has been paid in full by Him who now reigns on the throne of heaven. He "canceled the note that stood against us, with its requirements, and has put it out of our way by nailing it to the Cross" (Col. 2:14, C. B. Williams). And now He is sending forth "his angels with a great sound of a trumpet, and they shall gather together His elect from the four winds, from one end of heaven to the other" (Matt. 24:31; see also Mark 13:27). What has been said above about the sign of the Son of man in heaven and His coming in judgment upon Israel is proof that this sending of the angels is not in connection with the second coming.

In the Greek New Testament, the word *angelos* is translated either *angel* or *messenger*, according to the context. There are many instances in the King James Version where the Greek *angelos* or *angeloi* is translated *messenger* or *messengers* (see Matt. 11:10; 24:31; Mark 1:2; Luke 7:24; 9:52; James 2:25). From the day of the giving of the great commission until the day of His second appearing, Christ's followers will be the messengers or angels gathering the elect from all the nations of the earth. This is not an "end time" responsibility, but an "all time" mission during the whole of the gospel age, while the Messiah reigns on His throne in heaven. Indeed, in II Peter 3:9–10, Peter clearly indicates that this gathering time of the elect is during the time between the ascension and the second appearing. And the Lord's coming is delayed until that work is done.

But what about the sending of these messengers "with a great sound of a trumpet"? (Matt. 24:31). The trumpet was the common means of getting the attention of the people for any important matter, whether it be the call to the new year observance, or the approach of an enemy army (Num. 10:1–2). Our Lord was using this background of Hebrew experience as a prophetic symbol of His messengers calling out the elect from the four corners of the earth during the gospel age. The Lord's assurance, just three verses ahead, that this would happen in the lifetime of His hearers absolutely prevents us from referring it to the future time when the last of the saints are called home.

THE CERTIFICATION OF THE PROPHECY

The first section of our Lord's prophecy closes with a positive certification of its meaning.

The Parable

First Jesus gave the parable of the fig tree, assuring His disciples that they could read the signs of His predicted destruction of the temple, as one would read the signs of the times. "Now learn a parable of the fig tree: When his branch is yet tender, and putteth forth leaves, ye know that the summer is nigh: so likewise, ye, when ye shall see all these things, know that it is near, even at the doors" (Matt. 24:32–33; see also Mark 13:28–29; Luke 21:29–31).

Luke introduces this parable of the fig tree with the words: "When these things begin to come to pass, then look up, and lift up your heads; for your redemption draweth nigh" (Luke 21:28). Here is the assurance that the temple's destruction would bear the message that the glorious redemption through the Messiah was at hand. Since the temple came into existence to bring about this very thing, the followers of the Lord Jesus could now understand that the temple functioned as only the preparatory to gain the permanent.

The Pledge

Second, came the Lord's double attestation: "Verily I say unto you, This generation shall not pass, till all these things be fulfilled. Heaven and earth shall pass away, but my words shall not pass away" (Matt. 24:34–35; see also Mark 13:30–31; Luke 21:32–33). Could anything be plainer than that the entire prediction of the Lord leading up to this point was to be fulfilled in the lifetime of His disciples? He staked His sacred honor on it. How, then, dare we contradict or attempt to circumvent His words? When these things predicted are properly understood, secular as well as sacred history witnesses to the fact that "all these things" happened in that generation. To superimpose upon "these things" a measured seven year tribulation still future, or a so-called pre- or post-tribulation second coming, or a regathering of the Jews to Palestine, or a millennium, is to do violence to the Word of the Lord.

The study of Israel's great tribulation again impresses us with the fact that the almighty God turns the afflictions brought about by the efforts of Satan into glorious victory through Christ. God's way of developing an eternal kingdom of joy is the way of the cross.

THE SECOND APPEARING OF JESUS

At this point in our Lord's Olivet prophecy the subject changes from "those days" to "that day" (Matt. 24:36; Mark 13:32; Luke 21:34). As we indicated on page 47, "the day, that one" sets it apart as a particular day, a day of special significance above other days. And this section limits itself to that day. The only appearance of "days" is in the illustration about Noah, and is equivalent to "time" (Matt. 24:37–38).

In this second section we have our Lord's fullest teaching regarding His second appearing recorded in the Gospels. Previous to this, He had surprisingly little to say about His second coming. That is understandable. His death and resurrection were necessary before His disciples could grasp the significance of His second appearing. As full as this teaching is, our Lord does not mention a secret rapture, a seven year tribulation, a regathering of the Jews, or a millennium, in connection with His coming.

The Day

"But of that day" rivets our attention to the great day of consummation. More than fifty times in the New Testament, "that day," or "the day," or "the last day," or "the day of the Lord Jesus Christ," or "the day of God," or their equivalents, point to the second appearing of Christ. "That day" is described as the "day of visitation," or the "day of judgment," or the "day of wrath," or the "day of redemption," or the "great day." Some interpreters attempt to find more than one day indicated by these references, as for instance a radical difference between the "day of the Lord" and the "day of Christ." But this only leads to confusion and the necessity of manipulating Scripture to justify such interpretation. The day of the Lord Jesus Christ, made possible by the day of His crucifixion and the day of His resurrection, will be the greatest day, the climactic day, of redemptive history.

The Time

"But of that day and hour knoweth no man, no, not the angels of heaven, but my Father only" (Matt. 24:36; see also Mark 13:32). We shall not attempt to explain the Son's surprising ignorance. That remains one of the many mysteries of His incarnation. In spite of this, history tells us of many date-setters, who evidently think they are wiser than the Son of God or the angels.

It should not surprise the faithful Christian that the time of our Lord's coming is unknown. "A future event, which combines these two things, absolute certainty that it will happen, and utter uncertainty when it will happen, ought to have power to insist on being remembered."[7] But what sort of servant is he who has no glow of gladness at the thought of meeting His Lord?

The Son of God will come at an unexpected time.

---

[7]Alexander Maclaren, *The Gospel of Matthew,* p. 169.

> But as the days of Noe were, so shall the coming of the Son of man be. For as in the days that were before the flood they were eating and drinking, marrying and giving in marriage, until the day that Noe entered in the ark, and knew not until the flood came, and took them all away; so shall also the coming of the Son of man be (Matt. 24:37–39).

There was no need for the people of Noah's day to be surprised, for they had been warned both by God's word and by Noah's work of preparing the way of escape. But so it is today, multitudes do not believe that clear promise of the Savior's unexpected return.

That means that Christ's second appearing will be a time of division. "Then shall two be in the field; the one shall be taken, and the other left: two women shall be grinding at the mill; one is taken, and one is left" (Matt. 24:40–41). Why this division? The ones taken will have a Noah-like faith that will be absent in those who are left. Another thing to notice here is that there is neither the suggestion or the implication of a "secret rapture."

The three Gospels give the same advice in view of the certain coming of the Lord: "Watch therefore: for ye know not on what day your Lord cometh" (Matt. 24:42; see also Mark 13:35, 37; Luke 21:36).

Responsibility

Jesus closes His prophecy with a series of parables which indicate the nature of His coming and the proper response on the part of the faithful who are alert as they await His coming. The heart of His advice in each case is "Watch," be on the alert.

6

Tribulation of Antichrist, Man of Sin, and Satan

The adherents of the view that a seven-year tribulation will be experienced before or after the second coming of Christ depend much upon their teaching concerning the Antichrist, the Man of Sin, and Satan's "little season" of release. Therefore, we must examine the Scriptural teaching regarding these subjects.

THE ANTICHRIST

As we have pointed out in our discussion of Daniel's prophecy of the seventy weeks of remaining Jewish history, the dispensationalists not only separate the last week from the sixty-ninth by an unannounced gap of centuries, they even substitute an Antichrist for the Christ as the one who confirms the covenant and causes the sacrifice and the oblation in the restored temple to cease. We shall not repeat our reasons for rejecting this view; they are given in full on pages 48–49 and 58–59.

As a matter of fact, the word *antichrist* appears nowhere in Daniel's prophecy of seventy weeks. And it is found only four times in the entire Bible. The apostle John alone uses the word. What does it mean?

Does it imply that the power or party indicated by it should, in some form or another, arrogate Christ's peculiar office and work, or does it simply express a spirit of contrariety and opposition to His doctrine or kingdom? Nothing, in this respect, can be gathered with certainty from the word itself, for the preposition (*anti*), which is here used in composition with Christ, alike expresses formal opposition to an object, and the supplanting of it by taking its place; and there is a series of compounds, in which the one idea, and a series in which the other idea, is embodied. It is only, therefore, by the usage of the word, and the comparison of parallel passages, that we can determine in what specific sense it is to be understood, and what kind of contrariety to the truth of Christ it was meant to designate.

The first passage in St. John's epistle, by whom alone the word is used, stands literally thus: "Little children, it is the last hour (or season); and as ye heard that the antichrist cometh, even now many have become antichrists, whence we know it is the last hour" (chap. 2:18). Here there is no precise definition of what the term antichrist imports, but the assertion chiefly of a fact, that the idea involved in it had already passed into a reality, and that in a variety of persons. This, however, is itself of considerable moment, especially as it conveys the information that while the name is used in the singular, as of an individual, it was not intended to denote the same kind of strict and exclusive personality as the Christ. Even in the apostolic age John finds the name of antichrist applicable to many individuals. And this, also, may so far help us to a knowledge of the idea, since, while there were numbers in that age who sought within the church to corrupt the doctrine of Christ, and without it to disown and resist His authority, we have no reason to suppose that there were more than a very few who distinctly claimed the title of Christ, and presumed to place themselves in Messiah's room.

The next passage occurs very shortly after the one just noticed, and may be regarded as supplementary to it; it is in the 22nd verse. The apostle had stated that no lie is of the truth; and he then continues, "Who is the liar? (*o pseustēs*, the liar by preeminence) but he who denieth that Jesus is the Christ. This is the antichrist, who denieth (or, denying) the Father and the Son." Here it is the denial of the truth concerning Christ, not the formal supplanting of Christ by an impious usurpation of His office, to which the name antichrist is applied. Yet it could not be intended to denote every sort of denial of the truth, for this would have been to identify antichristianism with heathenism, and Judaism, and unbelief generally, which was certainly not the meaning of the apostle. The denial of the truth by the antichrist was made in a peculiar manner—not as from a directly hostile and antagonistic position, but under the cover of a Christian name, and with more or less of a friendly aspect. While it was denied that Jesus was the Christ, in the proper sense of the term, Jesus was by no means reckoned an imposter; His name was still assumed, and His place held to be one of distinguished honour. That this was the case is evident not only from the distinctive name applied to the form of evil in question, but also from what is said (in ver. 18, 19) of the originations of the antichrists. "Many," says the apostle, "have become antichrists"; they were not so originally, but by a downward progress had ended in becoming such. And, still further, "They went out from us, but were not of us;" that is, they had belonged to the Christian community, but showed by the course of defection they now pursued, that they had not formed a part of its living membership, nor had really imbibed the spirit of the gospel.

When, therefore, the apostle says in the verse already quoted, that those whom he designated antichrists denied Jesus to be the Christ; and when, in another verse (chap. 4:3), he says, "Every spirit that confesseth not Jesus Christ come (*elēlutota*) in the flesh, is not of God; and this is that spirit of antichrist whereof ye have heard that it should come (literally cometh), and now already is it in the world;" and, still again, when he says in his second epistle, ver. 7, "For many deceivers have entered into the world, who confess not Jesus Christ coming in flesh; this is the deceiver and the antichrist."

In all these passages it can only be of a virtual denial of the truth that the apostle speaks. He plainly means such a depravation of the truth, or abstraction of its essential elements, as turned it into a lie. And when further he represents the falsehood as circling around the person of Jesus, and disowning Him as having come in the flesh, we can scarcely entertain a doubt that he refers to certain forms of the great gnostic heresy—to such as held, indeed, by the name of Jesus, but conceived of Him as only some kind of shadowy emanation of the Divine virtue, not a personal incarnation of the Eternal Word. Only by taking up a position, and announcing a doctrine of this sort, could the persons referred to have proved particularly dangerous to the church—so dangerous as to deserve being called, collectively and emphatically, *the Deceiver*—the embodiment, in a manner of the old serpent. . . .

We arrive, then, at the conclusion, that in St. John's use of the term *antichrist*, there is an unmistakable reference to the early heretics, as forming at least one exemplification of its idea. Such, also, was the impression derived from the apostle's statements generally by the Fathers; they understood him to speak of the heretics of the time, under the antichrists who had already appeared. . . .

It is plain, indeed, that the existing antichrists of John, the abettors and exponents of the *pseudos*, or lie, under a Christian profession, the deniers of what is emphatically true, belonged to the very same class with the grievous wolves and false brethren of Paul, of whom he so solemnly forewarned the Ephesian elders, and of whom he also wrote in his epistles to Timothy (1 Tim. 4:1; 2 Tim. 3:1), as persons who should depart from the faith, teach many heretical doctrines, and bring in upon the church perilous times. John, writing at a later period, and referring to what then existed, calls attention to the development of that spirit, of which Paul perceived the germ, and described the future growth. The one announced the evil as coming, the other declared it had already come.[1]

The significance of the apostle John's writings on this subject must not be overlooked. As noted above he is the only New Testament writer to deal with the Antichrist by name. And he is the only New Testament writer to mention the thousand years (in Rev. 20), commonly referred to as the millennium. Why, then, we ask, did he fail to explain the chronological relationship of the Antichrist and the millennium? The answer seems self-evident to us: the two are not related. Antichrists, according to John, are present throughout the Christian age; there is no dated period when they are not present and active as enemies of the people of God. And the so-called millennium, according to John, is the period which we know as the gospel age when Satan, condemned already, is limited in his attempts to deceive the nations. John, himself, explains this in Revelation 1:18; 12:9; 20:1–8 and in the Gospel of John 12:23–33; 16:8, 11; 19:30.

The presence of antichrists throughout the gospel age conforms to our Lord's warning to His disciples: "In the world ye shall have tribulation" (John 16:33). And the church finds this to be its experience in an antichristian world.

---

[1]Patrick Fairbairn, *Prophecy*. (Edinburgh: T. & T. Clark, 1856), pp. 348–52.

THE MAN OF SIN

Paul's man of sin, or man of lawlessness, is identified as the Antichrist who will dominate the dispensationalists' *seven-year tribulation*, which will take place, they declare, between the removal of the Holy Spirit and the church from the world and the appearing of Christ. By thus postponing the Antichrist's influence, with the tribulation incident thereto, they rid all but seven years of the Christian era of one of its most exasperating characters. And this they do in spite of the fact that the Lord Jesus Christ and Paul and John characterized the church age as a time of tribulation marred by many antichrists.

Some of the Thessalonian believers had been disturbed by a report that Paul had said "that the day of the Lord is already here" (II Thess. 2:2, C. B. Williams). That meant, if true, that they had missed the coming of the Lord Jesus Christ and their final "muster before Him." Paul disabused their minds of this false report by assuring them that Christ's coming and their "gathering together unto Him" could not take place until two very definite things happened:

> Let no man deceive you by any means: for that day shall not come, except there come a falling away first, and that man of sin be revealed, the son of perdition; who opposeth and exalteth himself above all that is called God, or that is worshipped; so that he as God sitteth in the temple of God, shewing himself that he is God. Remember ye not, that, when I was yet with you, I told you these things? And now ye know what withholdeth that he might be revealed in his time. For the mystery of iniquity doth already work: only he who now letteth will let, until he be taken out of the way. And then shall that Wicked be revealed, whom the Lord shall consume with the spirit of his mouth, and shall destroy with the brightness of his coming: even him, whose coming is after the working of Satan with all power and signs and lying wonders, and with all deceivableness of unrighteousness in them that perish; because they received not the love of the truth, that they might be saved. And for this cause God shall send them strong delusion, that they should believe a lie: that they all might be damned who believed not the truth, but had pleasure in unrighteousness (II Thess, 2:3–10).

In this prophecy of Paul, we find three things about the man of sin: his revelation, his description, and his activity.

Revelation of the Man of Sin

At the time of Paul's writing, the man of sin had not been revealed, although "the mystery of iniquity" was already at work. This man of lawlessness would not be revealed until "there come a falling away first." Soon thereafter, if not immediately, he would appear on the scene. History proves that a great apostasy from the true faith soon developed, as John's statements about the "many antichrists" seem to evidence. Hence, we have every right to conclude that the man of sin has for many centuries been active. While there is in the passage no indication of the length of his activity, it is definitely declared that it will be brought to an end at the second appearing of the Christ, when that wicked one shall be consumed "with the spirit of his mouth, and shall be destroyed by the brightness of his coming" (II Thess. 2:8). In the sacred record there is no suggestion of a seven-year limit to his reign of terror. Paul's words seem to indicate that the church age would largely be the victim of the work of the man of sin.

The power of influence restraining the open activity of the man of sin is not identified by Paul, although he had previously told the Thessalonians the meaning of what he later wrote. While this leaves us today without certainty as to the restrainer, we can be sure from historical evidence that this man of sin has been revealed over and over again in the past.

Description of the Man of Sin

First, he is the personification of lawlessness. Second, he is "the son of perdition," whose sin necessarily brings destruction. And third, his "coming is after the working of Satan with all power and signs and lying wonders, and with all deceivableness of unrighteousness in them that perish" (II Thess. 2:9–10). He is one of John's antichrists, perhaps the chief. The believers of that time would certainly be able to identify without difficulty this enemy of the Lord Jesus Christ.

Activity of the Man of Sin

First, he "opposeth and exalteth himself above all that is called God, or that is worshipped" (II Thess. 2:4). "Above" is to be understood in the sense of "against." He is the instrument of Satan.

Second, "he as God sitteth in the temple of God, shewing himself that he is God" (II Thess. 2:4). Remembering that this epistle was written to Christians, and not to Jews, "temple" must certainly refer to the church, for the dwelling place of God among His people was no longer understood as a sacred building in Jerusalem. God's earthly dwelling place had now become the church,

> built upon the foundation of the apostles and prophets, Jesus Christ himself being the chief corner stone; in whom all the building fitly framed together groweth unto an holy temple in the Lord: in whom ye also are builded together for an habitation of God through the Spirit (Eph. 2:20–21).

In other words, the man of sin is from among the professing Christians, who sets himself up in the church and poses as God. This interpretation is verified by the apostle John, who says of the "many antichrists," "They went out from us, but they were not of us; for if they had been of us, they would no doubt have continued: but they went out, that they might be made manifest that they were not all of us" (I John 2:19).

Third, in spite of his claims, his activities are "after the working of Satan with all power and signs and lying wonders" (II Thess. 2:9).

Who Is This Man of Sin?

The popular answer is that the man of sin is a future antichrist, to be revealed when the Holy Spirit and the church are taken out of the world at the rapture. He, they claim, will preside over a seven-year tribulation, at which time he will make a covenant with the Jews, only to break it, and cause the sacrifice and oblation of the rebuilt temple to cease. We cannot accept this answer, (please check this statement by the Scriptures), for it is pure speculation without a verse of Scripture to justify it.

We think history has the full and adequate revelation of the man of sin. Let us put it in the words of Patrick Fairbairn, one of the most competent of all interpreters:

> We cannot for a moment doubt, that it is there [in Romanism and the papacy] we are to look for the most complete, systematic, and palpable embodiment of its grand characteristics. *There*, we perceive, as nowhere else, either to the same extent, or with the same determination of purpose, a mass of errors and abuses "grafted on the Christian faith, in opposition to, and in outrage of, its genius and its commands, and taking a bold possession of the Christian church." We see "the doctrines of celibacy, and of ritual abstinence from meats, against the whole spirit of the gospel, set up in the church by an authority claiming to have universal obedience; a man of sin exalting himself in the temple of God, and openly challenging rights of faith and honour due to God; advancing himself by signs and lying wonders, and turning his pretended miracles to the disproof and discredit of some of the chief doctrines and precepts of Christianity; and this system of ambition and falsehood succeeding, established with the deluded conviction of men still holding the profession of Christianity" [Davidson]. All this meets so remarkably the conditions of Paul's prophecy, and in its history and growth also from the apostolic age so strikingly accords with the warnings given of its gradual and stealthy approach, that, wherever else the antichrist may exist, they must be strangely biassed, who do not discern its likeness in the Romish apostasy.[2] We may the rather rest in the certainty of this conclusion, as it is a matter of historical certainty that ages before the Reformation, and, indeed, all through the long conflict that was ever renewing itself on the part both of secular and spiritual opponents against Rome, the pope was often denounced as the antichrist, and man of sin. . . .
>
> But while we thus hold the charge to be applicable to the Romish church, primarily and peculiarly, we by no means think

---

[2]This was written before the infallibility of the pope and the assumption of the Virgin Mary had been made dogmas of the Roman church.

> that it should be laid there, as it too commonly is, exclusively. The
> Eastern church, which does not differ essentially from that of
> Rome, must also be included; and much, too, that is to be found
> under the name of Protestantism.[3]

Again, we see that the idea of a short seven-year great tribulation period just before or after the coming of Christ fails the
scriptural test. The whole period of human history, from the
first man to the last, is the great tribulation. God's people are
constantly persecuted and called upon to suffer for Him. Their's
is the way of the cross.

SATAN'S LITTLE SEASON

Satan is ever and always a persecutor during the entire period
of the great tribulation. But Revelation 20:1–10 shows that after
the thousand years of Satan's binding he "must be loosed a little
season." It is definitely stated that this loosing would be in order
that he might "deceive the nations . . . to gather them together
to battle." "The battle," it is generally agreed, is the final conflict
between good and evil, also called Armageddon (Rev. 16:13–21;
19:17–21).

When will Satan's little season of future activity occur? The
answer has been given above: After the thousand years of his
binding. But that raises another question: When do the thousand years occur? Some answer confidently: At the future
coming of the Lord. Others say that his binding took place at
Christ's first coming and he will not be released for this "little
season" until the thousand years are about to end. Which answer is correct? It seems to me that we are forced back to the
cross for the true answer—the place where we find all the answers to sin's problems. The *when* of Satan's binding will be
clear when we understand *what* that binding was for.

What was the binding of Satan for? The following Scriptures

---

[3]Patrick Fairbairn, *Prophecy*, 2nd ed. (Edinburgh: T. & T. Clark, 1865), pp. 369–70.

give the answer. I John 3:8: "For this purpose the Son of man was manifested, that he might destroy the works of the devil." How did He destroy those works? Hebrews 2:14: "He also himself likewise took part of the same [flesh and blood], that through death he might destroy him that had the power of death, that is, the devil." This was the binding of Satan symbolized by what John saw, as recorded in Revelation 20:1–3:

> I saw an angel come down from heaven, having the key to the bottomless pit and a great chain in his hand. And he laid hold on the dragon, that old serpent, which is the Devil, and Satan, and bound him for a thousand years, and cast him into the bottomless pit, and shut him up, and set a seal upon him, that he should deceive the nations no more, till the thousand years should be fulfilled: and after that he must be loosed for a little season.

If you ask John to identify the angel of his symbolism he does that in Rev. 1:18: "I am He that liveth, and was dead; and, behold, I am alive for evermore, Amen; and have the keys of hell and of death." Clearly, the cross was the means by which Satan was overcome and bound. "Having spoiled principalities and powers, He [Christ] made a show of them openly, triumphing over them in it [the cross]" (Col. 2:15). That was what Jesus meant when He cried from the cross, "It stands finished, and is for ever done" (John 19:30, my interpretation). Just before He defeated Satan at the cross He told His disciples that the Holy Spirit would come, "And when He comes, He will bring conviction to worldly people . . . about judgment, because the evil ruler of this world has been condemned" (John 16:8, 11, C. B. Williams). Satan is now in chains waiting the execution of his condemnation. The *when* of his binding could have been at no other time. To put it at some future date discredits the cross, denies the statement of Jesus, "It is finished," contradicts the Holy Spirit's conviction that the ruler of this world is condemned, and calls upon the Lord Jesus to do over again what He completed during His incarnate and sacrificial ministry.

Hence, one of the periods of tribulation to be expected by mankind will be that period when Satan goes forth again to deceive the nations. It will be the time when Satan is making his last fight for power. When will it be? Nobody knows. Some are suggesting that the world has already reached that time. How long will it be? Nobody knows. The Word only says, for "a little season." But from this we see that Satan will attempt by all the power the Lord will allow him to have to finish what he started in the Garden of Eden.

7

Tribulation and the Christ

The coming of the Son of God to the world to atone for man's sin met with the shameful reception prophesied by Isaiah: "He is despised and rejected of men; a man of sorrows, and acquainted with grief: and we hid as it were our faces from him; he was despised, and we esteemed him not" (Isa. 53:3). Men heaped insults upon Him, and at last hounded Him to the cross. The cross of Christ is the last word in the record of tribulation's most ghastly crime; and it is at the same time the emblem of heaven's greatest victory. We must conclude from this that our God, in some mysterious way that we do not understand, uses tribulation and apparent failure as the strange instruments with which He wins His victories. Certainly cruel death became the victory of our Savior, our Example, our Teacher, our Lord.

OUR SAVIOR

"The eternal purpose which God purposed in Christ Jesus our Lord" (Eph. 3:3, 11) was made known to the apostle Paul by special revelation. And in his report of a divine, precreation council of the Trinity, in Ephesians 1:3–14, Paul tells us what that purpose was. It was a five-fold purpose.

Chosen to Solve Love's Supreme Problem

The first man's fall had broken mankind's love relationship to his Maker, and had defaced the image in which he was created (Gen. 1:27). This God could not tolerate, for "God is love" (I John 4:8, 16).

So we read in the letter to the Ephesians of the divine council, convened "before the foundation of the world," that it was God's good pleasure, "which he hath purposed in himself, that in the dispensation of the fulness of times he might gather together in one all things in Christ, both which are in heaven, and which are on earth, even in him" (Eph. 1:9–10). Thus, God Himself determined to solve love's problem in the person of His own beloved Son. "For God so loved the world that he gave his only begotten Son, that whosoever believeth in him should not perish, but have everlasting life" (John 3:16). The *measure* of God's self-giving love was a cross.

In a Lost and Unfriendly World

The world into which the Son of God came to do His work of love had already lost its faith in God, except for the few who believed in the promised victory of the Seed of the Woman (Gen. 3:15). Men had given Satan the allegiance of their hearts (Luke 4:6). "The course of this world," or the spirit of the age, was controlled "according to the prince of the air, the spirit that now worketh in the children of disobedience" (Eph. 2:2).

This heavenly restorer of God's love is declared to be the creator of all things. "For by him were all things created, that are in heaven, and that are in earth, visible and invisible, whether they be thrones, or dominions, or principalities, or powers: all things were created by him, and for him" (Col. 1:16). The tenants of this earth, then, would be expected to dethrone Satan and to welcome the Creator. Not so! "He came into His own world, but His own people did not welcome Him" (John 1:11, C. B. Williams). He was compelled to wrestle for man's soul "not against flesh and blood, but against principalities, against powers, against the rulers of the darkness of this world, against

spiritual wickedness in high places" (Eph. 6:12). His friends
were few; His enemies many. King Herod tried to kill Him before He was two years old. The people of His home town, after
hearing a Sabbath message from Him in the synagogue, "were
filled with wrath, and rose up, and thrust him out of the city,
and led him unto the brow of the hill whereon their city was
built, that they might cast him down headlong" (Luke 4:28–29).
The Jewish religious authorities in Jerusalem, custodians of the
written revelation of God, leaders of the temple worship, and
the ones offering the many bloody sacrifices that pointed to the
Lamb of God, the final and sufficient offering for all sinners, not
only rejected Him and turned the people against Him, but
crucified Him.

Self-denial—the Price of Success

How could the love relationship between a righteous God and
sinful man be restored? Paul reveals that the precreation divine
council of the Trinity decreed that sinful man would be redeemed and forgiven and brought into unity with his Maker
through Christ's blood (Eph. 1:7, 10). This meant that the Son of
God must so deny Himself as to take the place of the sinner just
as if He were the sinner, and endure death, the sinner's full
penalty for breaking God's law. Or, as Paul puts it in II Corin-
thians 5:21: "Him who did not know sin, for us He was made sin
in order that we on our part may become God's righteousness in
connection with Him" (R. C. H. Lenski).

> Behold Him, on the cross, bending His sacred head, and gather-
> ing into His heart in the awful isolation of separation from God,
> the issue of the sin of the world, and see how out of that accep-
> tance of the issue of sin He creates that which He does not require
> for Himself, that He may distribute to those whose place He has
> taken.[1]

That is true self-denial and perfect love.
No wonder He cried out from the hell of His suffering, "My

---

[1]G. Campbell Morgan, *The Crises of the Christ* (New York: Revell, 1903), p. 299.

God, my God, why hast thou forsaken me?" (Matt. 27:46). Forsaken! Earlier some of the members of His family forsook Him. Nazareth, His home town, forsook Him. The nation He came to save forsook Him. In every such instance He could always steal away to the tender, healing fellowship of His heavenly Father. In every such instance—until now! Now, God turns from Him. He withdraws the sunlight. He withholds His loving counsel. We can be sure that this was the strangest and most painful experience of anyone in all the universe.

Glorious and Eternal Victory

Christ's suffering on the cross is time's supreme demonstration of how our God makes "all things work together for good to them that love God, to them who are the called according to his purpose" (Rom. 8:28). It was by dying a cruel death that the Savior "abolished death, and brought life and immortality to light" (II Tim. 1:10).

It was determined by the Trinity, as reported by Paul in Ephesians 1:3–10, that "in the dispensation of the fulness of times God might gather together in one all things in Christ, both which are in heaven, and which are on earth, even in him." And this was to be accomplished "through his blood." John, the prophet, gives a preview of this accomplishment in Revelation 7:9–17:

> After this I beheld, and, lo, a great multitude, which no man could number, of all nations, and kindreds, and people, and tongues, stood before the throne, and before the Lamb, clothed with white robes, and palms in their hands; and cried with a loud voice, saying, Salvation to our God who sitteth upon the throne, and unto the Lamb. ... And one of the elders answered, saying unto me, What are these who are arrayed in white robes? and whence came they? And I said unto him, Sir, thou knowest. And he said to me, These are they who came out of great tribulation, and have washed their robes, and made them white in the blood of the Lamb.

> Wherefore God also hath highly exalted him, and given him a name which is above every name: that at the name of Jesus every knee should bow, of things in heaven, and things in earth, and

things under the earth; and that every tongue should confess that Jesus Christ is Lord, to the glory of God the Father (Phil. 2:9-11).

Unspeakable Joy for God and Man

Yes, the sacrifice Jesus made on the cross brought unspeakable joy to sinners who trusted Him as their substitute. But how can one say that that suffering was a joy to God? I don't know. It is a mystery. But in Ephesians 1:3-10, setting forth the precreation purpose of the Trinity, the motive behind that purpose is twice said to be "the good pleasure of his will." Williams translates one of the statements as "the happy choice of His will." And we find Paul describing the gospel to Timothy as "the glorious good news of the happy God" (I Tim. 1:11).

Still another passage adds to the mystery. It speaks of Jesus, "who for the joy set before Him, perseveringly endured (the) cross, despising (the) shame, and has sat down at the right (hand) of the throne of God" (Heb. 12:2, Lenski). Lenski explains:

> "The joy lying before Him" is the glorification that followed the sufferings plus His kingship over all believers. *Anti* expresses exchange: in order to get this joy Christ paid the price of the Cross with its shame.... During His entire humiliation, especially when He was foretelling the Cross, Jesus referred to His resurrection and the enthronement with the Father.... " Despising (the) shame" does not mean that the shame was a small thing, but that, in comparison with the joy, Christ scorned to consider it.[2]

Without asking for an explanation, all this gives a picture of heaven that is glorious indeed. All who dwell there possess an unspeakable happiness provided them by their Elder Brother, who allowed nothing to prevent Him from having the joy of saving them, and who rules the universe with a happy Trinity whose self-giving love is infinitively perfect. "The torture that was designed to degrade Him has set upon His Name a glory that can never vanish or fade" (F. W. Boreham).

---

[2]R. C. H. Lenski, *The Interpretation of the Epistle to the Hebrews* (Columbus, OH: Wartburg Press, 1946), pp. 428-29.

This, at least, puts the whole matter of tribulation in a different light. If it is the means of my salvation and the giver of a superior joy, I must welcome it as an instrument of God designed for eternal good. And with confidence I shall sing with the psalmist, "In thy presence is fulness of joy; at thy right hand there are pleasures for evermore" (Ps. 16:11).

OUR EXAMPLE

Not only did our Lord Jesus Christ qualify as our Savior by His suffering on the cross for us, He also is our example in demonstrating the use we shall make of our tribulations.

Jesus—Our Example of Self-denial

The classic passage on this subject is Philippians 2:5–10. Look at the paraphrase of this passage by J. B. Lightfoot:

> Reflect in your own minds the mind of Christ Jesus. Be humble as He was humble. Though existing before the worlds in the Eternal Godhead, yet He did not cling with avidity to the prerogatives of His divine majesty, did not ambitiously display His equality with God; but divested Himself of the glories of heaven, and took upon Him the nature of a servant, assuming the likeness of men. Nor was this all. Having thus appeared among men in the fashion of a man, He humbled Himself yet more, and carried out His obedience even to dying. Nor did He die a common death: He was crucified, as the lowest malefactor is crucified. But as was His humility, so also was His exaltation. God raised Him to a preeminent height, and gave Him a title and a dignity far above all dignities and titles else. For to the name and majesty of Jesus all created things in heaven and earth and hell shall pay homage on bended knees; and every tongue with praise and thanksgiving shall declare that Jesus Christ is Lord, and in and for Him shall glorify the Father.[3]

Doubtless some readers are saying, "How can I follow the example of Jesus as given in this passage? I cannot follow Him in

---

[3]J. B. Lightfoot, *Saint Paul's Epistle to the Philippians*. (London: Macmillan, 1908), p. 110.

laying aside the God-likeness I do not possess and taking on the human likeness I already have." No, you cannot. But you can have the same objective. Through the help of the Holy Spirit, you can become like Jesus in purpose and disposition and progressively become more and more like Him (II Cor. 3:18). You can take up your cross and follow Him, in self-sacrifice, as He commanded (Luke 9:23).

Jesus—Our Example in Obedience to God

Jesus boldly challenged His opponents, "Who of you can prove me guilty of sin?" (John 8:46). "I do always those things that please him [the Father]" (John 8:29). "I and my Father are one" (John 10:30).

> We find nowhere in His history, as we do in the case of the best of men, even the most occasional expression of the consciousness of sin; there is no humbling of Himself before God on account of sin—there is no prayer for the forgiveness of sin. Does not this inevitably lead to the conclusion that the source from whence those feelings, which we find precisely in the men of the highest moral character, proceed, had in Him no existence whatever? . . . There can therefore be no doubt that Jesus bore within Him the consciousness of being sinless and holy; and that to this consciousness He gave repeated expression. If we will not acknowledge the validity of a self-testimony of so peculiar a character; if we will not in simplicity lend our confidence to those sublime words, there remains nothing for it, but to declare Jesus to have been either a fanatic or a hypocrite, . . . a victim to the vainest self-deception. . . . Was Jesus then a sinner, and alone ignorant of the fact? . . . Such conclusions are too absurd to be entertained.[4]

In the sacred record, we find unexpected testimonials of His character. The Roman judge three times delivered the verdict, "I find no fault in this man." Judas Iscariot, who betrayed Him, confessed, "I have sinned in that I betrayed innocent blood" (Matt. 27:4).

Christ's followers, after His resurrection and their instruction

---

[4]C. Ullmann, *The Sinlessness of Jesus.* (London: T. & T. Clark, 1858), pp. 94, 105–106.

by the Holy Spirit, did not hesitate to testify that He was perfect in His obedience to God. "For we have not an high priest who cannot be touched with the feeling of our infirmities; but was in all points tested like as we were, yet without sin" (Heb. 4:15). He was "without blemish and without spot" (I Peter 1:19). They charged the Jews with denying "the Holy One and the Just" (Acts 3:14. See I Peter 3:18; I John 2:1, 29). And "He that saith he abideth in him ought himself also so to walk, even as he walked" (I John 2:6). "For even hereunto were ye called: because Christ also suffered for us, leaving us an example, that ye should follow in his steps" (I Peter 3:21).

Jesus—Our Example in Resistance to Satan

In discussing this point, we limit ourselves to two experiences in the ministry of Jesus: one His temptation by Satan in the wilderness, the other His agony in the Garden of Gethsemane; one at the beginning of His ministry, the other at the end.

Jesus used the Sword of the Spirit as His weapon in the fight against Satan. Each attack of the devil was countered with "It is written," "It is written again," and "For it is written" (Matt. 4:1–11). The Old Testament Scriptures gave Jesus God's word for what should be done when tempted to give the physical priority over the spiritual, or to justify the means by the end, or to give allegiance to anyone but the Lord God. And He won the battle.

In the Garden of Gethsemane, the Lord Jesus met Satan's assault with earnest agonizing prayer to His heavenly Father: "O my Father, if this cup may not pass from me, except I drink it, thy will be done" (Matt. 26:42). After three appeals, He came away triumphant over Satan's effort to keep Him from the cross.

Believers must follow the Savior's example for victory. God's Word not only makes us wise unto salvation, it is "profitable for doctrine, for reproof, for correction, for instruction in righteousness, that the man of God may be perfect, throughly furnished unto all good works" (II Tim. 3:16–17). And in prayer, we have the Lord's promise that the Father will answer with victory:

"Verily, verily, I say unto you, Whatsoever ye shall ask the Father in my name, he will give it you. . . . For the Father himself loveth you, because ye have loved me, and have believed that I came out from God" (John 16:23, 27).

We are not left to copy His example in our own wisdom and strength. He lives to make intercession for us (Heb. 7:25). And the Holy Spirit "maketh intercession for us with groanings which cannot be uttered" (Rom. 8:26). Thus the Trinity works for us in resisting the world, the flesh, and the devil.

Jesus—Our Example in Response to Need

Jesus responded effectively to every conceivable human need. Here, of course, we humans find it impossible to measure up to His standard. But two responses of Jesus will, at least, show us the lengths we should go in trying to imitate Him.

The first example is that of the healing of the leper (Matt. 8:2–4). This leper seems to have felt that Jesus had power to heal him, but was uncertain about His willingness: "Lord, if thou wilt, thou canst make me clean." And after his healing, the leper, whether deliberately or carelessly, disobeyed the Lord's strict order that he say nothing to anyone about the healing until he had reported to the priest. Both the faith and the obedience of this leper were defective. Here is an example of the Lord responding willingly to a need even when the one having that need might have been considered undeserving of His help. For that matter, who is deserving of the Lord's help? But, if we are to be like Him, we are obligated to meet the needs of men regardless of their deserts, in so far as we are able.

The second example was that of the dying thief on his cross. Jesus was in agony on the cross next to him. But He heard His companion's painful cry: "Jesus, Lord, remember me when thou comest into thy kingdom" (Luke 23:42). Quickly the suffering Savior answered, "Today shalt thou be with me in paradise" (Luke 23:43). Which would seem to say to believers that they should respond with the last ounce of their living energy to the need of men who are guilty of all but total neglect of Christ's claim upon their lives.

Jesus—Our Example in Demonstrating Love

Jesus' love is love that suffers long and is kind, envies not, vaunts not itself, is not puffed up, does not behave itself unseemly, seeks not its own, is not easily provoked, thinks no evil; it rejoices not in iniquity, but rejoices in the truth; it is the love that bears all things, believes all things, hopes all things, endures all things; it is the love that never fails; it is the greatest of all abiding things.

Never forget that this was a demonstration of the love that believers are to exercise, for He said, "This is my commandment, That ye love one another, as I have loved you" (John 15:12).

OUR TEACHER

Jesus Christ is not only our Savior and our Example, He is our Teacher. We are called disciples, pupils in His school. We are also called bondservants, slaves to do His pleasure. Did He instruct His disciples, His bondservants, concerning tribulation's part in the Christian life? Yes. A searching of the Gospels will amaze us with what He taught on this subject. We shall not attempt to give all that He said, but consider several of His teachings where suffering or tribulation is involved.

The Carnality of Human Nature

The Lord reminded His disciples that their sin-tainted nature might lead them into serious trouble if not repressed. His advice was drastic:

> If thy right eye offend thee, pluck it out, and cast it from thee: for it is profitable for thee that one of thy members should perish, and not that thy whole body should be cast into hell. And if thy right hand offend thee, cut it off, and cast it from thee: for it is profitable for thee that one of thy members should perish, and not that thy whole body should be cast into hell (Matt. 5:29–30; see also 18:8–9; Mark 9:43–48).

Of course the Lord was here using figurative language. But the eye is often the gateway through which evil enters the mind, and the hand is often the instrument that does the evil. This, then, is a warning that our carnal nature, attempting to shield us from suffering for Christ's sake, must be dealt with severely, even though the action hurts. The early disciples often suffered much more from yielding to their carnal nature than they might have from suffering for Christ. Peter found it so (Matt. 26:31–35; Mark 14:27–31; Luke 22:31–38).

The Enmity of the World

When He sent the Twelve, and again the Seventy, to the "lost sheep of the house of Israel," Jesus warned them, "Behold, I send you forth as sheep in the midst of wolves.... Ye shall be hated of all men for my name's sake" (Matt. 10:16–22; see also Luke 10:3; 21:19). Later, on His way to Gethsemane and the cross, He declared, "In the world ye shall have tribulation: but be of good cheer; I have overcome the world" (John 16:33). And, "If the world hate you, ye know that it hated me before it hated you. If ye were of the world, the world would love his own: but because ye are not of the world, but I have chosen you out of the world, therefore the world hateth you" (John 15:18–19). In His prayer to the Father, recorded in John 17:14, the Son of God declared, "I have given them thy word, and the world hath hated them, because they are not of the world, even as I am not of the world." The early disciples, basing their conclusion on this teaching of their Lord and on their personal experience (II Tim. 3:10–12), considered anyone who compromised with the world and its ways as an enemy of God: "Know ye not, that friendship of the world is enmity with God? Whosoever therefore will be a friend of the world is the enemy of God" (James 4:4).

The Secret of Blessedness

Perhaps we can say that our Lord, in His Sermon on the Mount, revealed the secret of true happiness. Let us give the substance of what He said: Happy are the spiritually poverty-stricken who want that condition changed; happy are the ones who mourn because of sin, theirs and others; happy are the humble, seeking God; happy are the hungry and the thirsty for heavenly righteousness; happy are they, who like Jesus, are merciful peacemakers; and happy are the persecuted in the service of the Lord (Matt. 5:3–12). All their needs shall be satisfied. They belong to the society of the prophets. And best of all, "Theirs is the kingdom of heaven" (Matt. 5:3, 10).

The Law of the Higher Life

On four occasions the Lord Jesus, in almost the same words, announced the law of the higher life: "Whoever wants to save his own life will lose it, but whoever loses his life for me and for the gospel will save it" (Mark 8:35; see also Matt. 10:39; Luke 17:33; John 12:25). The meaning is self-evident: "Sacrifice, self-surrender, death, is the condition of the highest life; selfishness is the destruction of life" (B. F. Westcott).

This law of life, announced so forcefully by the Lord Jesus, raises questions that every Christian should carefully consider: What was my understanding of the meaning of being saved? Did I wish merely to be saved from the punishment of my sins and the inconveniences of this earthly existence? Was I in fact asking Jesus to save the very thing He demanded that I put to death? Did I fail to see that the commitment to Christ was a commitment to the death of the self-life, with the acceptance of any discomfort or affliction involved in that dying; and a full dedication to the Christ-directed life?

According to this law, welcoming tribulation for His sake shows that we hate the world and love the Lord. Shunning tribulation shows disobedience to the law of life.

The Cost of Christian Discipleship

Do modern church people, who see nothing wrong in "doing their own thing," know the true meaning of Christian discipleship? Jesus was very careful, immediately after Peter and the others recognized Him as the Messiah, to instruct them in the meaning of discipleship. "He said to them all, If any man will come after me, let him deny himself, and take up his cross daily, and follow me" (Luke 9:23). When other statements made by Him are added, you will see that being a true disciple is serious business. Note some of these statements: (1) Christ's disciple must *resign* the control of himself to the Lord: "Let him deny himself." (2) He must *renounce* creature comforts. He, unlike the foxes with their holes and the birds of the air with their nests, had "not where to lay His head" (Luke 9:38). (3) He must *relegate* kindred to second place, while putting Christ first (Luke 9:59–62), even when that appears that he hates his loved ones (Luke 14:26). (4) He must *recognize* and fulfill the demand that he be perfect even as the Father in heaven is perfect, in so far as he can with Christ's help (Matt. 5:48). (5) He must *refuse* to submit to every temptation even if it requires plucking out an eye, or cutting off a hand or a foot (Matt. 18:8–9). (6) He must *rejoice* in suffering pain for Christ's sake: "Let him die on his cross daily, and follow me" (Luke 9:23). (7) And he must *remain* steadfast in his obedience to the Lord: "He that shall endure unto the end, the same shall be saved" (Matt. 24:13). In other words, he must present his body a living sacrifice, holy, acceptable to God, which is his reasonable service (Rom. 12:1). "When Christ calls a man, He bids him come and die" (Bonhoeffer).

These seem to be drastic requirements to the self-centered person. They are. But face it, our Lord declared, "Whosoever doth not bear his cross, and come after me *cannot be my disciple*" (Luke 14:27, italics mine). Jesus insisted that His disciples count the cost of following Him:

> For which of you, intending to build a tower, sitteth not down first, and counteth the cost, whether he have sufficient to finish it? Lest haply, after he hath laid the foundation, and is not able to finish it, all that behold it begin to mock him, saying, This man began to build, and was not able to finish. . . . So likewise, whosoever he be of you that forsaketh not all that he hath, he cannot be my disciple (Luke 14:28–30, 33).

Did the Lord really mean what He said? Ask the rich young ruler. Jesus allowed him to go away sorrowing and unsaved, because he refused to sell all that he had and to follow Christ (Matt. 19:16–22).

The Lord assures us that it is worth all it costs to be His disciple: "And he said unto them, Verily I say unto you, There is no man that hath left house, or parents, or brethren, or wife, or children, for the kingdom of God's sake, who shall not receive manifold more in the present time, and in the world to come life everlasting" (Luke 18:29–30).

How would Jesus answer the question: Will the church pass through the tribulation?

The Path to True Greatness

When the disciples asked Jesus, "Who is greatest in the kingdom of heaven?" he surprised them by setting a little child in their midst, and saying, "Verily I say unto you, Except ye be converted and become as little children, ye shall not enter into the kingdom of heaven. Whosoever therefore shall humble himself as this little child, the same is greatest in the kingdom of heaven" (Matt. 18:1–4; Mark 9:35). Earlier, in the Sermon on the Mount, He had said, "Whosoever shall break one of these least commandments, and shall teach men so, he shall be called the least in the kingdom of heaven: But whosoever shall do and teach them, the same shall be called great in the kingdom of heaven" (Matt. 5:19). When the mother of James and John asked the Lord to give them prominent places in His kingdom, He indicated that true greatness was not that of the princes among the Gentiles who exercised authority over men. "But whosoever will be great among you, let him be your minister; and whosoever will be chief among you, let him be your servant: even as the Son of man came not to be ministered unto, but to minister, and to give his life a ransom for many" (Matt. 20:25–28). Later, at the Last Supper, by stooping to wash the disciples' feet, He demonstrated the attitude of the true servant. And still later, at the cross, the Lord Jesus went to the depths of the lowest service, which, in fact, proved to be the highest service ever rendered to mankind.

This teaching regarding greatness sets in bold contrast the

ways of the world and the way of God. The Lamb who was slain is worthy "to receive power, and riches, and wisdom, and strength, and honour, and glory, and blessing" (Rev. 5:12).

We have considered the teaching of Jesus with reference to the tribulations that will come to those professing His name. Now we ask, Did our Lord offer a test whereby we might determine whether or not our response to His teaching is well-pleasing to Him? Yes, He did. "If a man love me, he will keep my words: and my Father will love him, and we will come unto him, and make our abode with him. He that loveth me not keepeth not my sayings: and the word which ye hear is not mine, but the Father's who sent me" (John 14:23–24). The answer is both positive and negative. "If a man love me, he will keep my words." "He that loveth me not keepeth not my sayings." Love for Christ is the test. And another statement from Jesus enables us to understand the character of that love: "A new commandment I give unto you, That ye love one another; as I have loved you, that ye also love one another. By this shall all men know that ye are my disciples, if ye have love one to another" (John 13:34–35). Our love for Him and others must resemble His love for us. Therefore, it must be a cross-bearing love. To claim to love Him while refusing to suffer for His sake is, in effect, denying Him.

8

Tribulation and Christians

A careful reading of the New Testament may surprise us with the many things written about the believer's suffering for Christ's sake. Indeed, such a careful reading will convince us that all true Christians shall experience great tribulation but emerge from it into the tearless life of eternal joy with the triumphant Christ.

PASSING THROUGH THE GREAT TRIBULATION

Our Appointment

Paul learned that the church in Thessalonica was disturbed by the afflictions connected with their receiving the Word (I Thess. 1:6). And he sent Timothy "to establish and to comfort [them] concerning [their] faith" (I Thess. 3:2). Here is what he said: "That no man should be beguiled [fooled] by these afflictions: for yourselves know that we are appointed [set] thereunto. For verily, when we were with you, we told you before that we should suffer tribulation; even as it came to pass, and ye know" (I Thess. 3:3–4). The word *appointed* used by Paul is the same Greek word used by Luke in reporting Simeon's word to Mary: "This child is set for the fall and rising again of many in Israel"

(Luke 2:34). Too, Paul remembered that he was chosen by the Lord to suffer for His name's sake (Acts 9:17). Therefore, when he and Barnabas revisited the churches they had established on their first missionary journey, he exhorted them "to continue in the faith, and that ye must through much tribulation enter into the kingdom of God" (Acts 14:22). They must know that persecution was a normal experience for Christians. The Christian life is not a picnic, but a war. And all believers are commissioned soldiers in that conflict.

We must not take the *appointment* of King Jesus lightly. It is our vocation, according to Peter: "For even hereunto were ye called: because Christ also suffered for us, leaving us an example, that we should follow his steps" (I Peter 2:21). *Example* in the Greek is a late and rare word for "a writing-copy for one to imitate." And Philippians 1:29 says that suffering in behalf of Christ is one of God's gifts to us: "For unto you it is given in the behalf of the Christ, not only to believe on him, but also to suffer for his sake." This might be translated: "You have (graciously) been granted the privilege of suffering for Christ." Note the two gracious gifts: the gift of faith in Christ, and the gift of suffering for Christ.

All of this is eminently consistent with what the Lord said about the cost of discipleship. Just after Peter had declared his faith in Jesus as the Messiah of God, the Lord laid down His requirements of disciples. Let us paraphrase what He said: "If any man without exception will redirect his course to come after Me, let him deny himself (not something, but his whole self), and deliberately take up his cross daily, to die on it to self and the world, and follow Me, as his one and only example in all of life" (Luke 9:23). And "whosoever without exception doth not bear his cross, daily dying on it, and come after Me, in complete obedience, cannot, under any circumstance, be My disciple" (Luke 14:27).

Our Conflict

This "world," which God created to reflect His glory, is in rebellion against Him. "The whole world lieth in wickedness'

(I John 5:19), under the sway of Satan, whom men have accepted as their god (II Cor. 4:4). Therefore, the moment we turn from the world of sin and become "the children of God," this wicked world disowns us as enemies (I John 3:1). Our Lord explains it: "If the world hate you, ye know that it hated me before it hated you. If ye were of the world, the world would love his own: but because ye are not of the world, but I have chosen you out of the world, therefore the world hateth you" (John 15:18–19). That means that when we were born again we were born into a human environment dominated by Satan. Our new birth, in other words, brought us immediately into conflict with the world, the flesh, and the devil.

We should not be surprised at being considered soldiers, and urged to "fight the good fight of faith, lay hold on eternal life, whereunto thou art also called, and hast professed a good profession before many witnesses" (I Tim. 6:12).

> We wrestle not against flesh and blood, but against principalities, against powers, against the rulers of the darkness of this world, against spiritual wickedness in high places. Wherefore take unto you the whole armour of God, that ye may be able to withstand in the evil day, and having done all, to stand (Eph. 6:12–14).
>
> Be sober, be vigilant; because your adversary the devil, as a roaring lion, walketh about, seeking whom he may devour: whom resist stedfast in the faith, knowing that the same afflictions are accomplished in your brethren that are in the world. But the God of all grace, who hath called us unto his eternal glory by Christ Jesus, after that ye have suffered a while, make you perfect, stablish, strengthen, settle you" (I Peter 5:8–10).

"Thou therefore endure hardness, as a good soldier of Jesus Christ. No man that warreth entangleth himself with the affairs of this life, that he may please him who hath chosen him to be a soldier" (II Tim. 2:3–4). Some of Christ's soldiers suffer the loss of their lives for the cause. All true soldiers of the cross suffer hardships and wounds in the conflict.

Paul, Stephen, James the son of Zebedee, Mark, Luke, Barnabas, and all of the eleven original disciples, except John, were martyred in their devotion to the responsibility of serving Christ as His witnesses. Foxe's *Book of Martyrs* tells of many others who suffered death in resisting the world, the flesh, and the devil. Through the centuries Christ's martyrs have bloodied the pages of history. Today, Russia, China, and many mission fields have added to the number of the "souls of them that were slain for the Word of God, and for the testimony which they held." Companionship throughout eternity with these will be a privilege indeed. Or, will it be a bit uncomfortable for the many of us who "have not resisted unto blood, striving against sin"? (Heb. 12:4).

"How can we escape, if we pay no attention at all to a salvation that is so great?" (Heb. 2:3, Williams). This question was not directed to lost men and women, but to those who claimed to be saved while ignoring the responsibility of denying themselves and bearing their crosses daily.

Our Fellowship

Immediately after Peter confessed his faith in Jesus as the "Christ, the Son of the living God," the Lord announced that He would build a fellowship on the foundation of Christian faith in Him, against which "the gates of hell shall not prevail," and which would possess the keys of the kingdom of heaven. This fellowship Jesus called "my church," or "my assembly" (Matt. 16:15–19). This assembly, beginning with "about an hundred and twenty" members, was fully possessed and empowered by the Holy Spirit on the day of Pentecost, and grew from that day to a multitude today that no man can number.

> The one church . . . is the sphere of the action of the risen and ascended Lord. All its members are in Christ and are knit together by a supernatural kinship. All their gifts and activities continue the work of Christ by the power of the Holy Spirit, originate from Christ, and are coordinated by Him to the final goal. Then the Church will appear in the age to come as the one people of God united in one congregation before the throne, as the one celestial city—the new Jerusalem.[1]

This "church of God, which he hath purchased with his own blood," is the most important fellowship on this earth. It is

---

[1]William Chiles Robinson in *Baker's Dictionary of Practical Theology*, edited by Ralph G. Turnbull (Grand Rapids: Baker, 1967), p. 123.

God's army in the fight against Satan. Each soldier is a cross-bearer. Christ, the chief cross-bearer, is the Commander.

Peter addresses this select group, saying:

> Beloved, think it not strange concerning the fiery trial which is to try you, as though some strange thing happened unto you: but rejoice, inasmuch as ye are partakers of Christ's sufferings; that, when his glory shall be revealed, ye may be glad also with exceeding joy. If ye be reproached for the name of Christ, happy are ye; for the spirit of glory and of God resteth upon you: on their part he is evil spoken of, but on your part he is glorified. But let none of you suffer as a murderer, or as a thief, or as an evildoer, or as a busybody in other men's matters. Yet if any man suffer as a Christian, let him not be ashamed; but let him glorify God on this behalf (I Peter 4:12–16).

Paul lifts this suffering of the soldiers of the cross to the highest plane when he calls it "the fellowship of his [Christ's] sufferings" (Phil. 3:10). His meaning is explained by Colossians 1:23–24: "I Paul am made a minister; who now rejoice in my sufferings for you, and fill up that which is behind of the sufferings of Christ in my flesh for his body's sake, which is the church."

Paul does not mean that in some way he was supplementing the saving work of Christ. He meant that Christ continues to suffer in His members, who must lend Him their tongues, hands, and feet to carry forward the message of His salvation to the ends of the earth. This fact was impressed on Paul, who had been persecuting Christians, when he heard Christ say: "Why persecutest thou me?" And when they took the persecution that would have been heaped on Christ, had His body still been in the earth, they were, in a sense, filling "up that which is behind of the afflictions of Christ in his flesh for his body's sake, which is the church."

Peter assures us that we who have suffered for Christ's sake, will, when He shall come in His glory, "be glad also with exceeding joy" (I Peter 4:13). If you do not participate in that joy, why not?

Our Growth

When our heavenly Father takes tribulation or suffering, as a developing tool, and uses it in our case, it may not at the time be pleasant, but "afterward yieldeth the peaceable fruit of righteousness unto them which are exercised thereby. . . . Therefore, my son, despise not thou the chastening of the Lord, nor faint when thou art rebuked of him: for whom the Lord loveth he chasteneth, and scourgeth every son whom he receiveth" (Heb. 12:11, 5–6).

This was God's way with His only begotten Son. "Though he were a Son, yet learned he obedience by the things which he suffered; and being made perfect, he became the author of eternal salvation unto all them that obey him" (Heb. 5:8–9). And this is God's way with the rest of His dear children. Enduring hardness is the exercise that makes the athlete strong. And resistance to the world, the flesh, and the devil is the exercise that makes the believer strong.

Our Test

There are two possible ways of looking at trouble or suffering: one is to consider such as the means of hurt or failure; the other is to consider them as the vehicles of help and victory. The Christian attitude is the latter. Hear James, according to C. B. Williams's translation, say:

> You must consider it the purest joy, my brothers, when you are involved in various trials, for you surely know that what is genuine in your faith produces the patient mind that endures; but you must let your endurance come to its perfect product, so that you may be fully developed and perfectly equipped without any defects (James 1:2–4).

Paul's painful experience illustrates the truth of this.

> There was given to me a thorn in the flesh, the messenger of Satan to buffet me, lest I should be exalted above measure. For this thing I besought the Lord thrice, that it might depart from me. And he said unto me, My grace is sufficient for thee: for my strength is made perfect in weakness. Most gladly therefore will I rather glory in my infirmities, that the power of Christ may rest upon me. Therefore I take pleasure in infirmities, in reproaches, in necessities, in persecutions, in distresses for Christ's sake: for when I am weak, then am I strong (II Cor. 12:7–10).

Paul found that he could serve the Lord better with his thorn reminding him of his weakness, than without it. Its presence forced him to depend on the strength furnished by the Lord.

Our Lord allows our faith and devotion to Him to be tested again and again. We ought to be happy that innumerable instances arrive giving us the opportunity to prove that we belong to Him, until we can truthfully say, "I am persuaded, that neither death, nor life, nor angels, nor principalities, nor powers, nor things present, nor things to come, nor height, nor depth, nor any other creature, shall be able to separate us from the love of God, which is in Christ Jesus our Lord" (Rom. 8:38–39).

Thus by successfully meeting the various difficulties of our earthly existence that threaten our relation to our Savior, we prove that we will stand the test in the great final examination at the judgment. That is what Paul was saying in II Thessalonians 1:4–5: "So that we ourselves glory in you in the churches of God for your patience and faith in all your persecutions and tribulations that ye endure: which is a manifest token of the righteous judgment of God, that ye may be counted worthy of the kingdom of God, for which ye also suffer."

The believer's

> faith is not some fragile thing, to be kept in a kind of spiritual wool, insulated from all shocks. It is robust. It is to be manifested in the fires of trouble, and in the furnace of affliction. And not only is it to be manifested there, but, in part at any rate, it is to be fashioned in such places. The very troubles and afflictions which the world heaps on the believer become, under God, the means of making him what he ought to be.[2]

Our Joy

What is joy? The world certainly cannot tell us. "The natural man receiveth not the things of the Spirit of God: for they are foolishness unto him: neither can he know them, because they

---

[2]Leon Morris, *The First and Second Epistles to the Thessalonians* (Grand Rapids: Eerdmans, 1959), p. 198.

are spiritually discerned" (I Cor. 2:14). The world has destroyed the true meaning of joy by insisting that self-gratification is the secret of joy. Nothing could be further from the truth.

Paul astonishes us by insisting that both *joy* and *longsuffering* are the fruit of the Spirit (Gal. 5:22). Let him explain: "For I reckon that the sufferings of this present time are not worthy to be compared with the glory which shall be revealed in us" (Rom. 8:18). "For our light affliction, which is but for a moment, worketh for us a far more exceeding and eternal weight of glory" (II Cor. 4:17). Therefore he tells Timothy, "Endure hardness, as a good soldier of Jesus Christ" (II Tim. 2:3). And James adds, "Blessed is the man that endureth temptation: for when he is tried, he shall receive a crown of life, which the Lord hath promised to them that love him" (James 1:12).

There are so many references to real joy in the Scriptures that I will merely jot them down with a brief comment, leaving the reader to look them up in his Bible: Genuine joy is an attribute of God (Ps. 16:11; 104:31); the fruit of the Holy Spirit (Gal. 5:22); the gift of Christ (John 16:24); the result of Christ's work (Acts 8:8); the possession of the disciples (Acts 13:52; Phil. 2:2; I Thess. 2:19-20); the prayer of Jesus for His own (John 17:13); the companion of Christian suffering (II Cor. 6:10; Col. 1:24; I Thess. 5:16; Heb. 10:34); the duty of all Christians (Phil. 3:1; 4:4; I Thess. 5:16); and the highest possible experience of the one who has stood the test of suffering for Christ's sake (Acts 5:41; II Cor. 6:10; I Peter 1,6, 8; 4:13). It was in order to gain this joy that our Savior endured the cross (Heb. 12:2).

Refusal to deny self and to suffer for Christ will deprive us of this greatest of all joys. How, then, can we expect to rejoice in the things of heaven?

Our Opportunity

Certainly I have been writing about great opportunities: the opportunity to accept gladly a divine appointment; to engage in the world's most important conflict; to fellowship with Christ and Christians; to grow in grace; to have my faith tested; and to discover the means of true joy. But that is not all.

Willingly suffering in Christ's service gives us the opportunity of *demonstrating for God*. Once, when Jesus gave sight to a man who was born blind, His disciples asked Him, "Master, who did sin, this man, or his parents, that he was born blind?" (John 9:2). They evidently had not read the Book of Job, for they thought that affliction was always the result of sin. But Jesus answered, "Neither hath this man sinned, nor his parents: but that the works of God should be made manifest in him" (John 9:3). In other words, God allowed this to happen in order that Christ's power to bring sight to the blind might be demonstrated. Many of the afflictions experienced by Christians may not be due to sin, but may be allowed that men may see that God is able to heal the world's ills. This is another of our God's strange ways: using this man to demonstrate to parents, Pharisees, and many others, the power of God to bless through Christ. What greater service could one render?

Again, willingly suffering in Christ's service gives us the privilege of *representing Jesus* with authority. Paul without question was a true representative of Jesus. He tells Timothy: "For this cause I obtained mercy, that in me first Jesus Christ might shew forth all longsuffering, for a pattern to them which should hereafter believe on him to life everlasting" (I Tim. 1:16). The Greek word translated *pattern,* used here only in the New Testament, means *"sketch"* or *"rough outline."* Even if our sketch of Jesus is only a rough outline, this is the way the world gets to know Jesus. Such outlines are

> "always bearing about in the body the dying of the Lord Jesus, that the life also of Jesus might be made manifest in our body. For we which live are alway delivered unto death for Jesus' sake, that the life also of Jesus might be made manifest in our mortal flesh" (II Cor. 4:10–11).

By thus *representing Jesus* in His sufferings, we gain authority in witnessing for Christ. Only the one who has suffered for Christ's sake, has a right to be heard. He knows from experience what Christ can do. When he speaks, it is with the authority of one who has obeyed the Lord when it cost to do so.

Once more, suffering for Christ gives us the opportunity of

strengthening our hope of life eternal. Hope is an "anchor of the soul" and can be "both sure and stedfast" (Heb. 6:19). Paul tells us how to strengthen that hope progressively to the end: "We glory in tribulations also: knowing that tribulation worketh patience; and patience, experience; and experience, hope: and hope maketh not ashamed" (Rom. 5:3–5). Every one of us should welcome the tribulations that produce such results.

God, in His Word, has faithfully revealed the truth regarding the necessity of cross-bearing. Indeed, it is so emphasized that no one can fail to see its importance, except by ignoring or neglecting His Word.

EMERGING FROM THE GREAT TRIBULATION

One of the greatest scenes in the Bible is the word picture of the Savior's cross-bearers coming out of their trials into the capital city of "the kingdom prepared for [them] from the foundation of the world" (Matt. 25:34). This picture is found in Revelation 7. Let us examine it.

Context

The theme of Revelation is the triumphant Christ and His church. The book naturally divides itself at the end of the eleventh chapter into two parts. The first eleven chapters give three pictures of the work of the exalted Christ. He is seen as Prophet among His churches (1:12—3:22), as King on His throne (4:1—8:1), and as interceding Priest at heaven's altar (8:2—11:19). Since the rest of the book has to do with the warfare of the church, the body and bride of Christ, and does not directly affect the interpretation of Revelation 7, it is not necessary to deal with it here.

The seventh chapter of Revelation comes at the very end of the vision of the exalted Christ on His heavenly throne during the gospel age. It is a part of the sixth seal vision, presenting two contrasting companies: one made up of the high and low of mankind trying to hide from the wrath of the Lamb at the time of His second appearing (Rev. 6:12–17). The other company is made up of those able to stand in the day of the Lamb's wrath, for they have been sealed as Christ's own and have "washed their robes, and made them white in the blood of the Lamb" (Rev. 7:1–17). The first of these companies identifies itself as the enemies of Christ, and is of importance to our study only as representing the end of the lost contrasted to the never-ending triumph of the blood-washed.

Identification

The literalists, pointing to the 144,000 "of all the tribes of the children of Israel" in Revelation 7:4–8, insist that this refers to the elect from among the Jews; while the great multitude in Revelation 7:9–10 refers to the elect church from among the Gentiles. Other interpreters rightly reject this idea, insisting that there is only one group, symbolized in verses 4–8 as the New Testament "Israel of God," and in verses 9–10 as coming from "all nations, and kindreds, and people, and tongues." "The Israel of God" could not have been sealed by the Holy Spirit (II Cor. 1:22; Eph. 1:13; 4:30) without being washed "in the blood of the Lamb" (Acts 20:28; Rom. 5:9; Eph. 2:13; Col. 1:20; Heb. 9:14; 10:19; I Peter 1:18–19; Rev. 1:5; 5:9; 12:11). Nor could the "great multitude" have "washed their robes and made them white in the blood of the Lamb" without being "sealed by the Holy Spirit." Things equal to the same thing are equal to each other.

It would be to mar the consistency of the apocalyptic style, and introduce the greatest arbitrariness into its interpretation, if the tribes of Israel were here to be taken in their natural sense. Nor would it accord with the symbolical import evidently attached to these 144,000. It is against all probability to suppose, on the hypothesis of the literal reading of the passage, that precisely 12,000 of elect ones were to be found in each of the tribes specified. And if that improbability could anyhow be got rid of, why should only twelve tribes have been specified, and not thirteen, the actual number of the tribes? Is it to be conceived that, while each one of those twelve should furnish 12,000, Dan, the tribe omitted, should furnish none? The very omission of this tribe, so as to leave the historical number, twelve, and the precise squaring of this number, so as to make the twelve times twelve, multiplied by a thousand, shows that it is not the meaning of the letter we have to deal with, but the symbolical representation of a perfect and complete totality. This appears, also, from the object of the sealing, which was to stamp, with the sure impress of Heaven, "the servants of the living God," the Lord's people generally, as being through the Divine protection safe from the desolations that were to sweep over "the earth and the sea." The sealed are manifestly the representatives of all whom Divine grace saves from the world-wide judgments contemplated in the visions. . . . These reasons are still further confirmed, and rendered altogether conclusive by the subsequent reference that is made to the subject. In chapter 14 the Lamb is seen standing on Mount Zion with 144,000, the same sealed company "having His name and the name of His Father (so it should be read) written on their foreheads." These are described in terms that can only be understood of the elect generally, not of a mere fraction of the elect. It is said of them that they alone could sing the new song, and that they were virgins, faithful followers of the Lamb, redeemed from among men. They are, therefore, the saved; and appearing as representatives, forming an ideal number, and in a state of ideal perfection, they are also fitly called the first fruits unto God and the Lamb.[3]

Condition

This great multitude, composed of all the redeemed of all time, are standing "before the throne, and before the Lamb, clothed with white robes, and palms in their hands," singing the song of salvation, and, along with the angels, worshipping God (Rev. 7:9–12).

> Therefore are they before the throne of God, and serve him day and night in his temple: and he that sitteth on the throne shall dwell among them. They shall hunger no more, neither thirst any more; neither shall the sun light on them, nor any heat. For the Lamb which is in the midst of the throne shall feed them, and shall lead them unto living fountains of waters: and God shall wipe away all tears from their eyes (Rev. 7:15–17).

---

[3]Patrick Fairbairn, *Prophecy*, 2nd ed. (Edinburgh: T. & T. Clark, 1865), pp. 251–52.

Here is the fulfillment of God's purpose, made "before the foundation of the world," "that in the dispensation of the fulness of times he might gather together in one all things in Christ, according to the good pleasure of his will." These are God's adopted children, redeemed "through his blood," now at home with their heavenly Father and precious Savior (Eph. 1:3–14).

Experience

"Who are they?" and "Where do they come from?" one of the elders asked John. He must have known that the vision would be misinterpreted. John admitted that he did not know. So the elder answers (Rev. 7:14).

"Who are they? These are they... who have washed their robes, and made them white in the blood of the Lamb"—they who have understood the meaning of Christ's cross and have forsaken all to follow Him, regardless of the cost. There are no others in that throng before the throne. *Washed* and *made white* are both aorists in the Greek. "The aorists look back to the life on earth when the cleansing was effected" (Swete). Both Jews and Gentiles were there (Eph. 2).

Where did they come from? These are the ones coming out of the tribulation, the great one. *Coming* is a present middle participle with the idea of continued repetition: "They are coming." The significance of the two definite articles modifying tribulation has been explained on pages 12 and 13. It is the one great tribulation endured by all of God's people from Abel to the second coming, and includes all other tribulations of whatever severity and by whomsoever endured. All of them, grateful for "the mercies of God" had "presented [their] bodies a living sacrifice, holy, acceptable unto God, which is [their] reasonable service" (Rom. 12:1). Like Paul they could pray, "God forbid that I should glory, save in the cross of our Lord Jesus Christ, by whom the world is crucified unto me, and I unto the world" (Gal. 6:14). And many of them bore in their bodies the marks of the Lord Jesus.